CATCHING AN ORANGE

A CASE HISTORY

PRAISE FOR *CATCHING AN ORANGE*

"Amy Crider proves an unforgettable companion for a daring journey—through her own mental health, and a system that often fails her. *Catching an Orange* tells a story of blurred lines, a mysterious connection, and an unlikely triumph."

—Rob Walker, author of *The Art of Noticing*

"*Catching an Orange* is a vivid, absorbing, at times astonishing book. Startlingly honest and intimate, reading it feels like reading a stack of deeply moving personal letters found left behind on a Greyhound bus—letters meant for someone else but entrancing, revealing and affecting nonetheless. This book is not just a love story; it's many love stories overlapping and intertwined, which is how real life often flows. It has broadened and deepened the way I think about mental health challenges, and will stay with me for a very long time."

—Davy Rothbart, contributor to NPR's *This American Life*, creator of *Found Magazine*, and author of *My Heart is an Idiot*

"Once you begin reading Crider's utterly transfixing, vulnerable, and honest memoir, you won't be able to stop. Crider's stylish sentences investigate the space where brilliance and mental illness collide. Her story is heartbreaking and important."

—Amanda Eyre Ward, NYT-bestselling author of the Reese's Book Club pick, *The Jetsetters*

"Honest, gripping, heartbreaking."

—Jenny Lawson, bestselling author of *Furiously Happy*

"With piercing honesty and unexpected humor, Amy Crider reshapes the mental health memoir into something wholly original—intimate, fearless, and unforgettable."

—Julie Ryan McGue, author of *Twice a Daughter* and *Twice the Family*

"Sometimes, almost miraculously, a brief encounter with the right person can have a lasting impact on our lives. *Catching an Orange* is Amy Crider's moving ode to a therapist she only knew for three days, as well as an absorbing chronicle of her battle with mental illness during the latter years of the twentieth century. Her story shows us that even now, psychiatry is no match for the wonders and sufferings of the all-too-human mind."

—CHRISTINA PUGH, author of *The Right Hand*

CATCHING AN ORANGE

A CASE HISTORY

AMY CRIDER

GARRETT
COUNTY
PRESS

GARRETT
COUNTY
PRESS

CATCHING AN ORANGE

Published by Garrett County Press 931 N. Tonti Street New Orleans, LA 70119
Distributed by Simon & Schuster

ISBN (paperback): 978-1-939430-27-4

Library of Congress Control Number: 2025946737

Some names and identifying details have been changed to protect the privacy of individuals.

Book and cover design by Kevin Stone (https://good-design-is-good.com/)

Printed in the United States of America

First Edition

WORKS BY AMY CRIDER

NOVELS

Disorder

Kells: A Novel of the Eighth Century

STAGE PLAYS

Fourteen

Wells and Welles

CHAPTER ONE

Dear Dr. L.,

I have dreams about you. Dreams where I take your hand and say goodbye. You are always glad to see me. Your image is vivid. It is never like, "it was sort of you but you were a hydrangea." It is you, as you were thirty years ago, big brown eyes behind your glasses, soft, slightly babyish face and lips, tall in a double-breasted suit, an authority but with a touch of youth at the age of thirty-eight, with a serious look, concerned, hesitant to speak, and I wonder how certain you really were, or if you weren't really sure, of me, of the situation, of the diagnosis. You did seem sure, but were you?

I sat opposite you, my husband at an angle in the other chair, and you said I had a "physical problem causing dissociation."

I said, "You know me *so well*, after three days."

And with a nod of your head and a light tone that was unmistakably flirtatious, you said, "Yes, Amy, I *do*." It's not that I believe you'd fallen in love with me. It was only a moment, a special moment between us and for as long as I live, the memory of that quirky little moment will never cease to give me a warm glow. That warmth always suffuses my dreams of you.

I was so afraid of having nightmares as a child, that I would try to stay awake, yet I didn't have nightmares, only the one dream when I was eight: there were Valentine's cards on the table, a Saint Patrick's Day cake in the refrigerator, a Christmas tree in the living room, and no one would tell me what day it was. It wasn't the fear that people were keeping the truth from me. It was simply not knowing what was real. Alone, isolated in a dark house with the curtains drawn, I was the only person who didn't know what day it was, and not knowing the date meant not knowing what was real. That was the only nightmare of my childhood. If you had asked me even as a young child what my greatest fear was, I would have said: going insane.

To many people, there is a hard line between the sane and the insane. They need to feel that difference, to feel sure of their status. That issue of status is important. Mad people are contemptible, the bottom rung of society, provoking every negative reaction from annoyance to revulsion. At best, madness provokes pity, a contemptuous pity.

What do you think, Dr. L.? In your fine suits, your towering height, you presented such authority. Later I thought I loved you and wanted you, but then I realized, I wanted to *be* you. I wanted your knowledge, your authority, your confidence, your power. No one doubts the man in charge. No one mistrusts you, except of course the patients who need you, who need to trust you most.

No one, no layperson, feels entirely safe with psychiatrists. You're considered know-it-alls, smug, thinking you can read people's minds, thinking you know what's going on in people's heads. It makes people nervous. You have the status of the sane, but as a class that is adjacent to madness, you aren't beyond a certain aura of suspicion. I recall the trope of the mad psychiatrist from comedy television since my earliest childhood, back in the 1960s.

I'm safe, now, though. I never thought that I could live in a city, but here I am in Chicago, and every time we visit my in-laws in Indianapolis, they immediately ask, "Do you feel safe in Chicago? All the shootings? Do you feel *safe*?" Indianapolis has more murders per capita than Chicago, but Indianapolis isn't glamorous, and murder must have its glamour.

I'm safe here. In my warm bed, with the hum of traffic outside, I dream of you. Last night I dreamt I caught an orange. I was so happy, and I had to find you and tell you about it. You were there somewhere, and I had to tell you that I caught a ball for the first time in my life.

It's funny about dreams. When I was young, I always remembered them. I didn't understand when people talked about forgetting their dreams upon waking. There are dreams from my younger days I still remember vividly. Those days, I was a terrible insomniac. Now that I'm well and sleep normally, I often forget my dreams like a normal person.

I'm reading the obituary. You died on May 2. What was I doing May 2? It was a nothing day. No psychic feeling. No prophetic hawk on a branch. My last letter might have arrived right on that day. The letter before that, possibly the last one you read, ended with the line: "I think my letters to you are narratively exhausted," a conclusion so final, I almost feel like I killed you. I never meant to write to you for the rest of your life.

Your obituary (was it written by your wife, or your daughter?) mentions that conversations with you were always educational and enlightening; you were so well versed on many topics. Your necktie reflected your wide range of interests, the necktie you wore during our last conversation. Remember? A cool design of scientific formulas. You were talking about the need for medication. My husband turned to you, his eyes lighting up, "I *like* your tie."

He knew about many topics, too. It's funny how little over the years I wrote to you about him. The whole story sweeps over me now. I don't remember anymore how much I ever told you. Probably fragments, fits and starts. Now I'll try to organize it. How to tell it? Linear? Nonlinear? Meta? With foreknowledge? I'll have to feel my way.

I want to tell you everything, and you are gone. You are either in an omniscient afterlife, knowing all, understanding all, or somehow I must be satisfied with only the three days we knew each other, but I think there was a kind of omniscience between us, that we knew each other in some profound way, as if we were reunited from a former life when we were twin siblings who shared a secret language. Those three days were enough, because what you gave me still echoes, still teaches. I'll set it down before I forget, and then I'll tell you the wonderful dream about catching the orange.

CHAPTER TWO

I was having a horrible time in graduate school. It was 1984, and I was beginning a master's degree in history, but my BA was in an unrelated subject. I wasn't prepared, and my professors, who looked upon their roles not as teachers, but as judges, weren't interested in showing me what I was doing wrong, how to write a thesis statement, or what their vague assignments were asking of me. Years later, when I tried once again, a kindly professor said to me, "You seem to try to create the thesis in the mind of your reader." Exactly! He hit the nail on the head.

I didn't know that Bs were considered bad grades, and that Cs were failing. I just knew that somehow my teachers were angry with me for not knowing what I was doing; my ignorance offended their delicate view of academic *noblesse oblige*.

It wasn't as if I had a goal for this degree. It wasn't my ambition to become a professor. I was inspired to enroll after a conversation with an old friend. He had a degree in philosophy, and one night on the phone, as we discussed the world and politics, we kept running into our lack of knowledge about history. What had actually happened at this or that time, in this or that situation? I had a burning need to know. After two attempts to get the degree, I can say that a graduate program in history is not the place you will learn.

I don't even want to describe the soulless, bland basement-level apartment in the ticky tacky development, the screaming arguments of the couple next door, life without a car, confined to the classrooms, school library, and this tiny studio, no TV, no friends, no purpose. I was twenty-three years old.

I had come back to upstate New York because I'd spent my high school years there and thought the rolling dairy farm country was beautiful, but even this college town, Brockport, was flat and dull.

I had no family left in the area. My parents were in the Midwest and my siblings scattered around the country, so I was glad when an old friend from high school invited me for Christmas. She was married, and most of her family was still there, a few hours east of Brockport: her older brother, older sister, and parents.

Her brother was living with their parents, while her sister rented an apartment over their parents' garage. The sister, paying rent, was "independent," and their parents definitely noted the contrast between brother and sister.

I sometimes had dinner with them in high school. Their family prided themselves on eating around the dining table together every night, unlike mine eating out of our laps in front of the TV. They introduced me to fresh vegetables—broccoli, rutabaga—while my mother subjected us to cans of peas and a ghastly mixture called Veg-All. Except for salad, fresh vegetables were a mystery to my mother; I think she believed they took hours to cook.

In joining this family, I learned how to prepare beets. After rinsing off the dirt, boil them with the peel on. The dense vegetable takes time to cook. When they're done, cool until you can handle them, then rub off the peel under running water. The peel slips off in your fingers, and the water draining in the sink runs red, like the shower scene from *Psycho*.

While socializing with my old friend that Christmas, there was an easy compatibility between her brother and me. One moment especially stood out. I'd always been interested in filmmaking; my adolescent ambition was to direct. One night, as he drove his sister and me back from a movie, I was thinking how the sluggishly directed film was too long by about twenty minutes. Suddenly from behind the wheel he asked, "How much too long do you think that movie was, Amy? Maybe twenty minutes?" He'd read my mind.

When I first met him in high school, he told me that he identified as a Vulcan. It was the first thing I knew about him. He emulated Mr. Spock from Star Trek, explaining that Vulcans do have emotions, but they control them, using reason to control their emotions.

Like Mr. Spock, he was a vegetarian. He couldn't slaughter an animal himself, and wouldn't pay someone else to do it for him. Later I learned the actual impetus was his disgust when his mother served an undercooked chicken, pink juices running out.

He wore a fabric belt and canvas shoes to avoid leather. There were two things, though, he couldn't turn down at a restaurant or a potluck: French onion soup, which he didn't realize was made of beef stock, and Jell-O, which he simply couldn't resist. When we got engaged, I acquired cookbooks like *The Enchanted*

Broccoli Forest, and introduced him to imitation meats such as Grillers and artificial bacon bits. I got him to enjoy green peppers. Because he and his father, who had an ulcer, were convinced peppers must be hot, he had never tried them. His family loved vegetables, but we never could convince his father to try a pepper.

One night that week at his sister's, he joked about the "useless" literature class he'd been required to take in college, and I threw a French fry that hooked on his glasses. We all laughed. When he got home, he called me at his sister's. "Can we start over?"

We went to a movie at the mall, to see a silly comedy called *Johnny Dangerously*, and we kissed in the dark theater, his first kiss. I was a virgin, too. He was twenty-eight. When I went back to Brockport, he visited me on weekends. I bought a bed, and we both found a way out of our miserable loneliness. The romance was hot and my tiny studio was a love nest on the weekends.

I wasn't eager for a bigger commitment, though. At twenty-three, I had hardly begun my adult life. In my small basement studio, he stood in front of the ground-level window, his face shadowed in the light, his voice calm and contented with easy confidence, simply repeating: "We'll get married, though. You know we will get married. You know we're going to get married, anyway." It was a given, pre-ordained, something to be followed, not chosen. It was his expectation, his will, a force. Not demanding, not whining, but easy and calm and implacable. It was simply going to happen because he would not believe in any other reality.

I called my mother from a pay phone, hoping she would question it, hoping she would confirm my doubts. But I didn't come out and say my doubts. Instead I talked excitedly about the new romance and that we might get married.

"You always liked him, I remember," she said eagerly. She talked about the kinds of things that make people compatible. "If you go to bed and get up in the morning at the same time. All those little things." She thought my mind was made up. I was too excited for her to realize the doubts that shadowed me, that hummed like a distant sound. She, too, jumped enthusiastically on the bandwagon.

I recently had a dream in which he and I were at an airport. We were supposed to pick up my mother (she died in 2006). I was crying and pleading for how much I wanted my mother. It was a strange dream, because I have not felt a great deal of grief about my mother's death. At least, we didn't have unfinished business, and I haven't longed for advice or comfort from her over the years. Then it hit me: in the dream, I was grieving the mother I wished I had at the time, for a mother who'd question me and hold me back.

I emailed this to my sister. She said, "You were really starstruck with him. If mom had tried to hold you back, you would have married him, and would have resented that she didn't appreciate him." I told her no, that wasn't how I felt. Surprised, she said I certainly seemed like it at the time, that if I had any doubts I completely hid them from the world.

There were positive things of course: his humor, his kindness. He was handsome and truly charismatic, and he needed me. He had a certain glow about him, an aura. He helped me out, brought a car into my life, taught me to drive a standard shift. At the university learning center where I tutored, I was friends with an older student who was embarking on a difficult divorce while establishing a new relationship with another student. When she asked me why I was getting married, I said, "He makes my life easier." How she marveled at that! That a man could make your life easier!

As a writer, I was looking for my life to be like a novel. Reunited with him, this man I was attracted to years ago as a girl, would happen in a novel.

It was Fate. More than anything else, I had to go along with Fate.

He gave me security. This story, which will follow the journey of mental illness, psychiatric wards, and recovery, is perhaps more than anything else, a story about a lifetime of crippling anxiety. Anxiety that interfered with my jobs, silenced my speech, and kept me from feeling like an adult. And it wasn't really resolved until that night when I was already past the age of sixty, and dreamt I caught an orange.

CHAPTER THREE

There was something that drew me to him that was more compelling than his charm: his need to be loved. Even to be rescued.

He told me a story after we were engaged. We were in his bedroom at his parents' house in the afternoon on a sunny summer's day. He had been telling me how his mother never paid compliments, that they were all expected to get good grades, with no praise or reward. He spoke simply, without emotion.

"On my sixth birthday, when everyone was gathered for the party, I opened my gifts. My mom's was a gag gift. It was a baby bottle, to make fun of me because I drank soda out of the bottle. The whole party laughed, everyone laughed at me. I was six."

The desire to rescue someone is a deeply compelling emotion. There were things in my background that especially compelled me. I grew up with an alcoholic father, and my childhood in the 60s had this element of trauma:

When I was a child, a monk in Vietnam set himself on fire. This was my first knowledge of the outside world. My first fantasy of taking action in the world was of grabbing a blanket to smother his flames. When the "napalm girl" (Phan Thi Kim Phuc) was on the front page of the newspaper, she was nine and I was ten. Again, I longed to grab a blanket. This only reinforced a tendency to want to rescue people.

When we were reunited, I was adrift in life myself, so we were rescuing each other. The story of that party still haunts me. His mother's coldness was a dagger to his heart. It was true she let him continue to live at home while he worked odd jobs, but he also helped out his parents, doing maintenance on his father's rental properties. One day she criticized him for "sleeping the clock around," from ten to ten, which he vigorously denied. He was home because he dropped out of college due to suicidal ideation. But this was not an era or a place where a family would send their son to therapy.

His family considered him short-tempered, constantly harping on it, his red hair a sure sign of an angry temperament. He told me about "the dogs in the cellar." The anger pushed deep down inside, how he couldn't let the dogs out, a frightening anger he had to control. I never really saw him as short-tempered, because he didn't blow up at people. He blew up at things. If a tool broke, for example, if things didn't work the way they should, he'd get upset at the tool, at the object, but not at people. Over time I realized what his family saw as temper was really an extremely low tolerance for frustration. It was something he and I had in common, not being able to deal with frustration, and not being allowed to express anger.

That Christmas week, before we went on our first date to the movie, he invited me to his room to show me his great Invention. It was always The Invention. He took a sheet of paper and we sat at his desk—the desk he built himself. He drew a picture of a Van de Graff generator.

A Van de Graff generator has a dome that collects electrons, so that the current can be drawn off at a higher value than the current that was sent to it. At first, this sounds like "free energy," a generator that produces more energy than it consumes. Such a generator is impossible, it would violate the laws of physics. The reason that it doesn't produce free energy is because the electrons are brought to this dome on rubber belts which experience resistance. This resistance consumes some of the energy. No free energy.

But he had an idea. What if, instead of rubber belts, the electrons were sprayed into the dome by an electron gun, not unlike how televisions worked when they had tubes. This would eliminate the belts and the resistance. It would produce free energy.

Maybe my sister was right. Maybe I was starstruck. Because I allowed myself to believe in the possibility. I decided I was no expert in physics. Maybe he was a genius. Maybe the laws of physics needed to be rewritten, as they had been in the early days of quantum mechanics.

He was set on this idea making him a billionaire. And becoming a billionaire sounded good to me. He had already written to President Reagan about it.

He had an associate degree in engineering. When he started his BA, the university actually had a Van de Graff generator, but they wouldn't let him conduct his great experiment. His professors responded to his idea with a blanket statement that it couldn't work because of the laws of physics, but they didn't have the time or inclination to study it and say specifically why it wouldn't work. The fact that they wouldn't explain why kept his belief going. His depression that the university wouldn't let him prove his grand idea led him to consider plowing his car into the oncoming headlights at night. He left school and came home.

And now I was there to rescue this vulnerable, misunderstood man. He joked he was a "crackpot inventor," and I said he was a "mad scientist." I was on board. So many things can be true at once. My doubts, my hope my mother would slow this down, and yet my need to give him support and love, and my absurdly selfish belief maybe his invention was a million-dollar idea.

One of the authors of the physics textbook that had sparked the idea was named Zemansky. I don't know why this name stuck out to me. It stayed with me to the point that I made it the last name of the main character of my first novel.

There was certainly evidence he could do difficult things other people wouldn't attempt. One of the impressive things that stood out to everyone was that he built a car from scratch. Literally. He built the body from fiberglass, used a Honda engine, connected the drive train and everything. It had wing doors and he painted it yellow. It was registered as an "American homebuilt." I don't know how long he drove it, maybe a year. By the time I came along, it was off the road because it needed an engine repair. I never rode in it.

I didn't want a wedding because I was estranged from my alcoholic father. I didn't want him there, or much family there at all. We got married at the home of Justice of the Peace and school bus driver Buster Tilby, with a police scanner blaring in the background. I wore a chic thrift store dress and a new white hat. We had a gathering in his parents' yard. My mother-in-law baked a silver white cake.

CHAPTER FOUR

My husband enjoyed the idea of living to a very old age, in good health, with the advice of a book called *Life Extension*. It was all about taking vitamins and supplements, and touted the benefits of food preservatives. The authors were his gurus of health.

When we were first engaged, I had a job at a summer stock theater company near the Finger Lakes. We weren't living together, but he visited me early on for a weekend. The boyfriend of an actress was there, too, visiting from New York City, and she and I were both working as costume assistants that week. As the four of us chatted in the costume barn, I couldn't help noticing a certain masculine bent to the conversation.

The actress and her boyfriend were not fans of artificial anything. "They're finding Equal causes birth defects!" the actress declared with triumph. To my mind, discovering that an attempt to create an artificial sweetener might lead to the tragedy of birth defects was not something to *celebrate*.

My then-fiancé started touting vitamins, complaining about the fact that it was against the law for companies to put vitamins into soda pop.

The actress's boyfriend started questioning him about it. As he calmly asked pointed questions, not stating his own views, but questioning in such a deliberate manner, I realized he was baiting my fiancé. Winding him up, as the British say. He didn't care one way or the other about vitamins; he was playing a game.

I didn't say anything. I thought about responding by asking this young man if he were against putting vitamin D in milk. Cow's milk isn't a very natural thing for us to drink, and adding vitamin D is the only way to make the calcium useful. Would he oppose this? I never asked, but I've always wished I had.

A supplement that my husband was especially obsessed with was something called Co-enzyme Q-10. This was supposedly essential for heart health. He believed that one day when he was around twenty years old, while climbing nervously from a ladder onto the roof of his grandparents' house to help his grandfather with some repair, he'd suffered a heart attack. His arm felt numb and tingly, he felt a weight on his chest. Ever since, he believed that's what it was. His grandmother's brothers had all died young of heart attacks.

His health supplement Bible claimed that in Japan, when someone has a heart attack, they're always given copious amounts of Co-enzyme Q-10. So my husband took it as often as he could afford to buy it. I forget if it was ten or twenty dollars a bottle. His family usually gave him two bottles for his birthday or Christmas.

There was never any attempt to get his heart checked out. His father had an upper gastric ulcer, and sometimes his mother suggested he get checked for that, because it could have led to similar symptoms, apparently. But he just took his Co-enzyme Q-10 and insisted he was vulnerable to having a heart attack at any time.

Years later, around 1997, he did finally get an EKG. It indicated he'd never had a heart attack. He dismissed the results. "They only listened to four heartbeats," he said.

CHAPTER FIVE

That summer stock job didn't last. I was feeling especially stressed one day, between PMS, not sleeping well, and the whole time I worked there, my fiancé urging me to quit. He felt I "wasn't being paid minimum wage" because it was just the usual theater stipend. For some reason my having this job vexed him. I quit. I didn't understand until just recently how much he hated the idea of my working. He hated the idea of work, period.

At his first job, he was required to work unpaid overtime, and when he complained about it he was fired. Traumatized over this injustice, he made it his life's goal never to take a job he could be fired from again. He did handyman work and delivered newspapers—an adult's job in this rural area, as it required a car. He also had negative feelings about traditional work. "Why does everyone have to *work* for a living?"

he asked with a hint of rage. His father, who was in the semiconductor field for GE, often said how much he enjoyed his work and how lucky he felt, and never gave the impression he hated work, but my husband inveighed against the idea of slaving away, insisting his father was burdened with the hardship of dreary, exhausting labor.

We moved into an apartment owned by his father, getting a break on the rent in exchange for managing and doing maintenance. I got a part-time job at a drugstore and submitted short stories to as many magazines in the *Writers Market*—a gift from his sister—as I could.

I wanted to support my husband's dream to build his invention, and decided to become a high school social studies teacher. Two years into our marriage, I started a low-residency master's degree in education, with certification.

At the same time, we bought twenty acres of cheap land, parcels divided up from a farm. The farm was at the bottom of a hill, and we were thrilled to be up the hill with an amazing view of the valley to the south. The road rose steeply, and our parcel was a level area halfway up the hill before it rose again. There was an open field of maybe two or three acres, and the rest was wooded, with ash, copper beeches, and hemlock. Strangely, I almost never saw deer, though all the hills in the area were popular hunting grounds. Some nights we heard coyotes, which our neighbor called "coy dogs." There was a stream just inside the woods, and over the years I found numerous fossils of 400-million-year-old brachiopods. I still have a basket of them.

We asked the real estate agent about a perc test, a percolation test that shows whether the soil drains well enough to install a septic system. "It will perc," he said with the confidence of a man who knows he's lying. He repeated, "It will perc."

The land was hard clay, almost like concrete, and I knew an official perc test was chancy. There were two steps to getting a building permit, one for the township and one for the county. The one for the township was simple so we did do that. The one for the county would have required the perc test and other things. We didn't do that one. This never caught up with us; the one downside is that we never took the risk of protesting our grotesquely high property tax with the county. It was twelve hundred dollars a year, which might not sound like a lot, but the property with the house we built was only valued at thirty-five thousand dollars, so that was an incredibly high tax on such a low-value property.

This was about a 30-40 minute drive from his family in an isolated, rural area, dairy farming country. Except for a few years around my time as an undergraduate, I had lived in the area since middle school, and I loved the rolling hills, where I would walk for hours, looking for favorite birds and other nature friends: curious chickadees who flitted near if I stood still, tilting their heads to examine me. Grouse crashed upward through the trees on noisy wings. Tiny bright red newts with bulging eyes crawled out of the woods onto the road. A milk snake, white patterned with brown diamonds, lying on some random bale of hay fallen from a tractor. A mink crossing the road, limping awkwardly on its webbed feet like a little demon, chewing some creature in its maw. One day I found a great blue heron dead by a stream.

It was a euphoric day when we bought the land, as we walked the field of fallow grass and wildflowers, admiring the breathtaking view. We discussed a name for the property, such as Gallifrey, from *Doctor Who*. We never settled on a name. But I was relieved to get some distance from his family, and at least not live on the generosity of his father's apartment. There were certainly occasional comments about his older sister's "independence."

The only work we outsourced was hiring a backhoe operator to dig the foundation. My husband knew how to do things: carpentry, plumbing, electric. After he'd dropped out of college, he lived with his grandmother for a year in New Hampshire, making her old house livable. We agreed we liked "bumpy" houses, with old-fashioned cupolas or turrets, and then proceeded to design a plain rectangle, sixteen by thirty-two feet, because that was the most efficient way to use wood and sheetrock. The roof was dark green-finished metal. The propane gas stove had a built-in heater for the main floor. For the lower level, his brother-in-law gave us a small wood stove that had belonged to his father.

Doing all the work ourselves, much of it remained unfinished for years. The gray of unpainted sheetrock is still my least favorite color. It was many years later before I saw this pattern, his tendency to take on big projects and not finish them. He would sometimes take on handyman jobs and leave them unfinished, too, though not too often. Complaints slid off us, distracted by the stress of our poverty. At least no one sued him.

We moved into the house as soon as there was a shell. There was a kitchen sink and no bathroom. We had a plastic portable toilet we brought to his parents' house about once a week to empty.

We towed his yellow home-built car to the property, where it sat unrepaired for years. When it came time to move away, we had it towed to a junk yard.

I have a vague memory of something, from soon after we moved in. It was late in the autumn. His sister's best friend had left us a voice mail about some unfinished work my husband had done for them. They were remodeling their house, and he was supposed to build a couple of steps outside their back door. They'd been waiting a long time for him to do it. I tried to talk to him about getting over there to get it done. And he put up a strange resistance. I don't know what the problem was. He seemed distressed at the thought of doing it. He never did it.

I was starting to feel disturbed and depressed about things. His family had come over to see the house, and his mother's only comment was, "It's like Nana's. The floor sags." Nana was his grandmother in New Hampshire, whose house was a hundred years old. The beams holding up the floor of our new house were slightly understrength and sagged, which we fixed later. It was her only comment. Not, "Wow, you built a house!"

I felt disturbed by their relationship and was starting to feel overwhelmed by the amount of work left to do. When we got that voicemail from the woman about the unbuilt steps, and he wouldn't respond, I wrote a letter to her. I talked about the hardship of our lives. She wrote me a letter back about how hard it was for her, too, living with the dust of sheetrock as they remodeled. Our lives weren't comparable. She and her husband had good-paying jobs and were relatively well off, hiring all the work to be done on their house. She made it clear, though, that she was not prepared to sympathize. Of course, she was within her rights to be annoyed by the fact that all he needed to do was build two steps and for some reason wouldn't do it.

It's strange to remember how disturbed and depressed I was starting to feel. A memory of sitting in the living room at night, with only one lamp, the room all shadows. I wrote her another letter, not as coherent, something about how depressed we were, and how I thought there was something wrong with my husband's mother. And I remember clearly I had this fantasy, that this woman would get her priest (she was a devout Catholic) and just come to our place, just show up, to talk to us, to help us in some way, to listen to our distress and intervene in some way, at least emotionally. I really thought that could happen. Of course, I never heard back. That was the beginning of a long period of isolation.

CHAPTER SIX

My husband's interest in science and inventions of course made him a huge fan of shows like *Star Trek* and *Doctor Who*. His mother and sisters knitted him the long Tom Baker *Doctor Who* scarf from the official design. It's funny to look back on it all, at the time thinking of him as misunderstood and unloved, and see now the support and thoughtfulness they did show him, in these ways, making that scarf for him, giving him the Co-enzyme Q-10, letting him live at home for so long, employing him to work on his father's properties. Did my impression that he was unloved just come from him and his own sense of not being justly treated? Yet this brings to mind something my therapist said later in a different context, which I'll get to, about the difference between being indulged and being taken care of. They indulged him to a surprising degree without taking care of him in ways he really needed, such as encouraging him to see a therapist when he dropped out of school, or addressing the issue that he refused anything but marginal employment.

In terms of his interest in science fiction, years later, one of my brothers said something funny to me on the phone. "I turned on the TV and there was this crazy show on with this guy running around just like (my husband) going on about time travel and space and stuff." It was the Peter Davison *Doctor Who*. I didn't realize that except for his red hair, my husband looked quite a lot like Peter Davison.

He had an idea for another invention, a "lift disk," where a disk rotating in a vacuum would create thrust with minimal energy. He thought it could be used to make rockets to take people into space. He started making lists of people he would take into space with him. I asked him once why he wanted to go into space.

With a melancholy expression, he said, "Because nothing goes wrong in space."

He needed to test this by making a disk of wood rotate really fast, so he set up his circular saw to create the rotation. We stood across the room from it and he plugged it in. The saw whirled in a frenzy and the blade flew off toward our heads, smashing against the wall, a few feet from my neck.

I had a part-time job working for a potter, and my husband needed to generate a lot of heat to create the necessary vacuum for this idea. I don't know exactly what he was trying to do, but the potter loaned us a small, portable kiln made of steel. My husband packed insulation around it to get the super-hot temperature he needed, (this was actually the potter's suggestion). The steel lid of the kiln melted.

Meanwhile, I worked on my teacher certification. I had big dreams of what a good teacher I would be, exciting the minds of my students with the awe of knowing about the distant past, that we can know what people were doing, thinking, even *feeling*, a thousand years ago!

Student teaching was stressful. I discovered that social studies is frequently everyone's least favorite subject. They just weren't excited. I worked with two teachers; one, much more of a disciplinarian, was particularly unsupportive. And something was coming over me sometimes, something hard to describe. Soon after I finished student teaching, at the beginning of my final semester when it was time to finish my thesis, I experienced a strange, altered state for about ten days. I couldn't sleep. I had no appetite. My mind raced with philosophical ideas, about how our lives and everything we take for granted are social constructs.

I thought that speed and efficiency were destroying the world. I thought about Oedipus and how his tragedy was that his parents believed in the prophecy, believed in the Oracle, rather than their own son, the way a modern parent might believe in the calendar and the checkbook and the checklist more than their child. Oedipus was the story of crazy parents. I poured all my ravings into a notebook and wrote letters. As it wore on, I fell into silence, unable to speak.

I had suffered from insomnia for much of my life, not only voluntarily when I didn't want to have nightmares as a child, but increasingly since I was ten years old. In college I sometimes felt weird. One day as a freshman, I wrote a couple of poems and recited them aloud to myself for four hours. I attributed these mental states to lack of sleep. They were a rare occurrence, so rare I didn't think about them.

We didn't have kitchen cupboards yet in our unfinished house. In a burst of energy, I got some scrap wood, cut it to length with a handsaw, and nailed together a set of shelves. I had never done such a thing before, and it came out pretty good. It held our dishes for the next few years.

I lost the ability to read. Words seemed to evaporate from my mind. My husband could see something was wrong, though he didn't question me much. I promised him the only issue was that I needed to sleep, that if I could just get a good night's sleep, all would be well. It was too bad I promised this to him, because for years afterward whenever these states came back, he took this promise as an ironclad vow, wilfully holding me to it.

The final night of all this, I thought surely I was going to die, because I couldn't have such amazing philosophical revelations and still live. As I lay in bed, a cold breeze blew over me, and my breath got sucked away. I thought this was death. I cried out, waking my husband, to his annoyance. And then, it was over, as suddenly as it began.

I immediately made an appointment with my doctor, a general practitioner. I thought it possible I'd suffered a series of mini-strokes. When I went in for the exam and tried to tell him what happened, I spoke very slowly, exhausted. He tapped his clipboard and impatiently motioned for me to get on with it.

"Baby's coming," he said.

He had literally just been called to attend a childbirth but didn't cancel my appointment. He looked in my eyes with a light to determine I hadn't had a stroke, and diagnosed the occurrence as an "emotional breakdown" on my chart. He recommended a psychologist I couldn't afford.

He didn't tell me about the affordable county clinic, but later I discovered I could go there, where they had a sliding scale fee. I saw a young woman who was finishing her MSW degree, working to become a licensed therapist. I was diagnosed with bipolar disorder after a few visits, in January 1990.

The therapist said, "I'm diagnosing you as bipolar and we'll put you on chemotherapy."

The room tilted, the floor sank under my feet. It was disorienting to hear medication referred to as "chemotherapy." She meant the usual treatment of lithium carbonate capsules.

My therapist and I went to the staff psychiatrist, her boss at the county clinic who had to write the prescription. An old man with a thick German accent, he was partially deaf, and she shouted my symptoms at him: the manic episode, my depression.

I was using my maiden name then. He looked down at the forms and back up at me. "You're Russian?" he asked.

"My grandparents were."

He looked intrigued. "I'm from East Germany. I had to finish medical school under the Russians," he mused, a far-away look in his eyes.

He put me on the lithium. I had a follow-up with the therapist who explained I would get blood work to check my lithium levels every three months, and that she was leaving for another job. It was that quick. She said the nurse practitioner at the county health clinic could monitor my lithium. She offered to give me the names of some psychologists, "if you're still depressed," because the only other therapist at the affordable county clinic had a long waiting list, and I would have to go to the end of the line. There was no offer to make me a priority for that line. I knew I couldn't afford a psychologist outside the county clinic. That was it.

Decades later, I told a psychologist about it, as I finally understood how awful this was and how it changed me. He said, "You felt abandoned." I said,

"No, I *was* abandoned." It was a shock so deep, the impact was buried, as if I'd been secretly drugged and didn't realize it. Overnight, my bubbly, garrulous personality transformed, withdrawn into a dark void of shyness and acute fear of asserting myself. I'd always had issues with anxiety, but this was a tipping point.

I managed to finish my master's thesis and certification. I got the degree and looked for teaching work. Our rural area had a huge glut of teachers. I've never seen evidence of this legendary "teacher shortage" that I've heard about for forty years now. I did get a job, though, soon after the diagnosis, running discussion groups in high schools in a grant-funded drug prevention program. The weight of the diagnosis hung over me.

Since I now had insurance, I made an appointment with a psychologist. I wanted to talk about how it felt to have this diagnosis of a pretty major mental illness. Jovially, he asked, "Why do you care about this label?" It wasn't a label. It was an illness which had caused me suffering, and called into question all the decisions I'd ever made, my very view of who I was in the world. Unable to tell him how angry that question made me, I didn't see him a second time.

I consulted a psychiatrist. She was in charge of psychiatry at the local hospital. Her sharp chin, short reddish-brown hair, and glowing brown eyes made me think of a ferret, or a fox. An intimidating doctor, she expressed doubts that I was bipolar. The therapeutic range for blood lithium levels is 0.5-1.5. She decided my lithium should be at the minimum level, 0.5.

The nurse practitioner at the county clinic who was in charge of monitoring my lithium levels also questioned and undermined my diagnosis several times: "My brother is bipolar. You don't seem bipolar to me," she said. It was weird. What caused their doubts? Why were they undermining this diagnosis? My manic episodes and depressions were a textbook case of bipolar disorder.

I stumbled through life as best I could, not good at my job, the house unfinished, not confiding in anyone, barely making any friends.

It seemed like it was always winter. I drove to the schools where I worked over the empty country roads edged with ice, past snowy fields stubbled with cornstalks. The air was stiff, brittle, and crystalline. The houses scattered over the landscape were shut tight, tensed against the cold, the frigid world lonely and void.

The philosophical thoughts I had during the mania were not all delusional. I felt there was an inkling of something deeper, and I sought out spiritual guidance, with the goal of finding support for the ideas that weren't psychotic. In a bookstore I came upon a lovely hardcover edition of the Stephen Mitchell translation of the *Tao Te Ching*. It was exactly what I needed, and began an interest in Buddhism that continues today.

After some searching, I found a therapist who worked at the hospital. Her boss was the fox-woman psychiatrist who intimidated me. With her white hair, she seemed older, maybe in her late forties. She must have made a late-life career change, as she was still only a resident finishing her training when I started seeing her.

I had begun to think about leaving my husband, and much of our conversation was about this. For some reason, I didn't talk about the trauma of being diagnosed, the doubt it made me feel about my every decision, how it undermined my confidence. By then I had buried all that.

CHAPTER SEVEN

The property really was beautiful. There was a broad view of the valley to the south, with its hills of dairy farms. The tiny Unadilla River wound through the valley, where my brothers canoed in summers during high school with an artist friend, whose landscape painting of the Unadilla won first prize: the cover of *American Artist* Magazine.

Once on a cold, windy day in late spring, I was burning garbage behind the house and set fire to our field. I was terrified, but it was a low, cool fire, and the firemen mostly raked it out. That summer our entire yard was solid Queen Anne's Lace, born of the fire.

We had a little open porch, just a landing in front of the door. One autumn I set a couple of pumpkins on it. When they started to rot, I tossed them in the yard with a shovel, broke them up, and sprinkled them over with dirt. The following spring I had a pumpkin vine.

It was magical. When I told my dear old best friend, he said, "You accidentally invented agriculture."

Our social life consisted of visiting either my in-laws, or a good-humored, retired dairy farm worker who lived a short walk down the road. He had three sons in high school and his wife worked as a nurse. I would play chess with the oldest son. My husband would talk about his inventions, and the old man would tease us for our eccentricities. We laughed a lot with them. One thing I always remember was his rancorous view of his years as a dairy farm laborer. "You're a slave to cows," he said. "That's all it is. You're a slave to cows." I used that in the historical novel I wrote later about a farm in medieval Ireland.

It was fun to play chess with his son, the high school senior, because, though he was very smart, and certainly knew what he was doing, I would sometimes beat him. I'm not someone who understands strategy and can predict my opponent's moves. He explained I beat him because my moves were so erratic and crazy, he couldn't predict what I was going to do. In keeping with this era, I was the Ronald Reagan of chess.

Because of my family background with an alcoholic father and some other dysfunction, humor mattered. My family are all entertaining, jokey people. Though I did withdraw a lot after the diagnosis, I managed to continue to be funny and entertain when I was with familiar people. Those nights drinking coffee, playing chess, and joking around were a bright spot in our days.

In terms of my in-laws, while his parents' house was a usual meeting place, we also would drive to his sister's home in a farther town, an hour or so away. Her house was small, very dark and claustrophobic. It was among spindly trees on sandy ground that in ages past had been the bottom of a lake. In summer the mosquitoes and moths would loudly zap to their deaths in the many bug zappers. When her husband's family first bought the property, their father used DDT to clear the bugs every year, which was why it was a tolerable place to live when he bought it. The property was almost a swamp. I didn't like going there.

Our only other social interaction was an occasional drive to New Hampshire to visit Nana, my husband's grandmother. It was in a pleasant area, but there was nothing to do, and I felt oppressed by boredom. This was outside Concord. It seems very strange to me now that we never thought to explore Concord or visit a museum. We just sat around the house. We did once find the statue of Hannah Duston, a colonial ancestor of mine. My grandmother always made a big deal about her legacy, unpleasant as it was: after Native Americans kidnapped her and killed her baby during King Philip's War, she and another captive killed and scalped the whole band and escaped. For a long time she was a heroic figure in New England. Of course such a legacy is a bit different now. But I would talk about her in a braggy way, influenced by my grandmother. So we found her statue, and I got my picture with it.

Looking across from the statue, we noticed bales of something green next to a dark, low, foreboding building.

"Do you see those?" my husband asked.

"Yes, what are they?"

"Hides. It's a tannery."

We drove to Rye Beach on two visits, and one time Nana wanted to drive through the University of New Hampshire, where her son had gone to school. But we just drove through it, didn't park to get out and look around. My husband's family seemed contented to be in cars a lot.

Mostly we sat around her house, not doing much. I don't remember bringing a book with me to read. I don't know why not. She actually had a lot of books, ladies' novels from the mid-20th century. I like those novels a lot, but I didn't take one off the shelf to read. Many of them were published in their era, but you never see them in used bookstores. I think they've all been dumped in landfills now.

One day we went to a drugstore so I could buy a drawing pad, because the only paper Nana had was small stationery paper for letters. It seemed odd to me not to have paper, since our house overflowed with notebooks and drawing pads and typing paper. The drawing pad was to sketch costume and fashion designs, something I used to do for fun. Nana mentioned that my mother-in-law used to do the same hobby as a little girl, with a hint that one grows out of these things.

On another trip, I think somewhat later in our marriage, Nana mentioned something about my mother-in-law that struck a chord. My mother-in-law never understood the concept of algebra. It would come up humorously. "I still don't see how a letter can be a number," she'd say with a triumphant smile, as if we were all crazy.

She had a mysterious health issue when she was growing up. Eventually the diagnosis was that one of her legs was shorter than the other. Somehow this affected her health in baffling ways, including giving one doctor the impression something was wrong with her heart. This doctor gave the order that she must never get upset in any way. She was not allowed to be emotional, get angry, anything that would supposedly affect her heart.

So when it came time to learn algebra, which she could not understand at all, her older brother would tutor her at the kitchen table. Forbidden to get upset or express frustration, she sat with tears silently rolling down her cheeks. This image fills me with sadness. It was well into our marriage when Nana told us about it, and I couldn't help wonder whether this might relate to how my husband was raised with the constant criticism that he was short-tempered and not allowed to get angry.

CHAPTER EIGHT

In January of 1992, I had a holiday break from my job, since I worked on an academic schedule. My husband and I drove to Chicago to visit my old best friend from Goddard College, who was attending film school at Columbia College.

We stayed in his tiny studio apartment. I was surprised how cold Chicago was, as I avoided the icy puddles. My friend showed us a good time. We toured the Frank Lloyd Wright studio, and the two men let me browse the expensive gowns at Marshall Field's. We rode the el, the brown line which whipped around so close to the buildings downtown, that I was frightened enough to close my eyes.

My friend knew about a lot of things including the sciences. When my husband told him about his lift disk idea, my friend was skeptical. They set up a fan and a sheet of paper as my husband tried to explain how it would work.

We had enjoyed a long correspondence since college, where we were best friends. After we returned home from this visit, I wrote to him and expressed for the first time that I was wondering if my husband might be mentally ill. I don't remember how long I had been suspecting it. By then we'd been married almost seven years.

My friend wrote back saying he was wondering that, too. But then he continued to argue the finer points of my husband's lift disk idea.

This really angered me. I thought the whole topic of the lift disk or any other crazy invention was unimportant. My friend hadn't said a word of sympathy for the fact that I was married to a man who might be mentally ill. I wrote back in anger and said his response was "trivial and irrelevant."

This in turn enraged him. That was the end of our friendship for a long time.

At this time, my husband's mother was being treated for intestinal cancer that had invaded her liver. In the spring, a ten-thousand-dollar stent was inserted between her liver and intestine. I didn't think a doctor would go to such trouble and expense for a terminal case, so I thought her prognosis must not be bad. I underestimated the greed of doctors.

That April, we took a trip to London on my spring break. I had been working full-time in the drug prevention program for two years, and my husband also had a regular job for the first time, delivering packages for Airborne Express. It was a rare time in our marriage when we could afford this luxury. Just as we were about to board our flight, his mother took a turn for the worse, but this was before cell phones, and his family couldn't get the message to us not to go. She died three weeks after our return; we had a chance to say goodbye.

His family must have thought it selfish of me to plan this London trip when she was dying. She was pretending that she wasn't as ill as she was to let us go, a final gift. I've wondered whether the fact that I had decided we should take this trip to London when she was dying was the beginning of a secret hostility my husband's family began to feel for me.

I was becoming manic during the London trip, barely speaking. At the time, I was involved in an amateur play production, and the stress triggered obsessive thoughts. I fell very ill, and did something terrible. Before I go into it, there is something I'd forgotten until now, about the day she died.

We were all gathered in the hospital room while his mother breathed her last, unconscious and on morphine. From the next room thundered a man's loud, continuous retching, and I thought, *hell must sound like this*. Sitting with his back to the dying woman in the bed, her son-in-law chatted irrelevantly with the minister about China. Nana sat tearfully beside me at the foot of the bed. My mother-in-law had faced her cancer with grace and humor. I looked up at my sister-in-law, who was standing over the bed, and said that I respected how their mother faced her illness these past two years. Just as I spoke, my sister-in-law took her mother's wrist and felt for the pulse. She was dead.

A nurse quickly came in and ushered us out of the room. My husband and I went to the cafeteria to sit with a cup of coffee. We had arrived in separate cars and he left, but I had this strong feeling that she shouldn't be left alone. That at this moment she was alone in the room and needed someone beside her.

I went back alone to the hospital room. Her body had already been wrapped up in a white sheet, tied with a white cord. I sat, watching over her for a few minutes. I wondered if what I'd said about respecting her in the end were the last words she heard, though she was probably unaware of anything by then. I felt a sense of forgiveness, and a sense of making a promise that I would watch out for my husband, her son.

But I was becoming manic, had been since the London trip. The family brought her body home to New Hampshire for burial. I was working, so I didn't go with them.

My husband returned to the house in the afternoon from New Hampshire. Manic, losing my grip on reality in a way more serious than ever before, I didn't realize it was the same day as his return from burying his mother. I literally thought it was now weeks later. I said I was leaving him. I was becoming psychotic and said delusional things, things I'm ashamed of, and I kept repeating in a chanting, mindless way, "Feed the hungry child within you." I still feel horrible. I can't fault his family's anger over it, despite my bipolar excuse.

There was something else, something I've never admitted to anyone. I'd been thinking about his parents, how his mother was cold and cruel to him. It occurred to me his father had never intervened in this, didn't seem to defend him. His father let him drop out of college and live at home, but hadn't tried to get him psychological help. We had a complicated relationship with his parents because of my husband's work for his father's rental properties. One day my sister-in-law told me their father had complained behind our backs about "supporting two families," how he resented my husband's dependence on him.

I replied that, in a way, their father was the one who was dependent on my husband to do this labor for him. I don't like that it got framed this way at all; the reality was the arrangement benefited both of them. But after I said that to his sister, though it was never discussed by anyone afterward, their father never hired him again.

So, that terrible day when I told my husband I was leaving, I also said I thought his father didn't love him. That's what I'm ashamed of beyond anything. He had just returned from burying a mother he'd had a strained relationship with, and for me to say that I thought his father didn't love him was the most horrible thing I could possibly say. Then I continued to repeat, "Feed the hungry child within you."

Everyone knew I was bipolar. My husband had seen it before, not as bad as this, but bad enough.

Didn't he suspect I was deluded by mania? He didn't question me, barely said a word. He got up and drove to his parents' house to tell his family I was leaving him, and report on everything I had said, as if I were sane. He said nothing to them about the possibility I was manic.

Later, when I was better, I complained to my therapist about his ignoring my mania to go to his family. She said he would have been hurt, angry, and confused. He needed his family on his side.

Thinking it over right now, I wonder if perhaps what I said about his father not loving him was mitigated by his immediately going to see his family. Maybe he got some needed assurance from his father that he was loved. Maybe it afforded something positive. Is that possible? We never discussed it afterward; I'll never know.

This was my only experience with that kind of dissociation, ripped out of time, floating in a dream, not aware of what day it was or how much time had passed. That night I abruptly woke from the fog, and realized it was the same day as his return from burying his mother. I sank to the floor on my knees, shaking, horrified to have lost touch with reality. It was terrifying. Reality had crumbled away from me, like an object in some sci-fi movie turning to dust in one's hand.

The shock of recognition ended the episode.

I tried to tell his family of my horror. His brother-in-law casually said that it was "terrible timing" for me to say I was leaving when I did, as if I were normal, as if the whole thing was normal. Though my husband had seen me manic before, his family had never witnessed my symptoms, which had now passed. It was impossible to make clear that I wasn't in reality when this happened, that it was horrifying, a living nightmare. It was literally my childhood terror of going insane come true.

They seemed not to hear. I felt like a foreigner with a broken language.

CHAPTER NINE

The week that my mother-in-law died, I lost my mother too, in a different way. When I was manic that awful day, insights mingled with delusions came with a thunderbolt: the mother I'd always idolized might not be what I thought. Memories of weird things about her hit me. Wandering a cul-de-sac as toddlers without supervision. My brother falling and cutting his forehead while watching a construction site when he was five. What was he doing there alone at the age of five?

In 1949, when my mom was nine, her two-year-old brother fell out of a moving car and was killed. When I was a child, there were times when my car door wasn't shut all the way. Mom would slow down rather than stop, and have me open and slam shut the door, without a seat belt on. Every time we passed a dead robin on Rimmon Road, Mom would stop to take it out of the street to keep it from getting squished. So many dead robins on that stretch.

I went to my therapist, fresh from waking from the horrible nightmare of dissociating, and said I thought my mother was crazy and I was crazy too, aside from being bipolar.

The therapist said, "You have a dissociative disorder because your mother has a personality disorder."

I had not talked much about Mom in therapy, and I asked the therapist how she knew this about her.

She replied, "You never talk about your mother. Therefore you are protecting her. Therefore she has a personality disorder."

I slid off the chair and sank to the floor of her office, shaking and crying. Joyous, glowing about my revelation, my therapist said, "I feel like I'm with a baby, all pink and new."

She asked if my grandfather was a secret alcoholic. Because my father drank, she thought my mother had married him because my grandfather drank. It was unlikely. Grandpa was active in the community and worked on a master's degree at night. The next week as we continued to go over it all, she said eagerly, "And you said your grandfather secretly drank," as if the idea were mine and not hers. That startled me;

for a moment the room shimmered and grew fuzzy.

It occurs to me now that it would have been perfectly appropriate to hospitalize me over all this. I had dissociated. I was delusional. It would have made sense. And if I had been hospitalized, I might not have lost my job, which was another consequence of the episode. The optics for my husband might have been awkward, to take me to a psych ward and say, "My wife just told me she is leaving me..." but it would have been the right thing to do. It's too bad no one thought about it at the time.

I thought I needed to get well before making a big decision about leaving. Clearly I was not a sane person, and every decision I'd ever made seemed suspect. I decided to stay another year and see how things stood then. This was another bad decision, as if there were anything positive in making a promise with a deadline on it. At the time it felt reasonable to me, but it wasn't at all.

Sometimes in life, you do the wrong thing, and you don't get to feel forgiven, you just have to live with it, and go on and sin no more.

When you're ill this way, it's not like you black-out. You remember everything you said and did, and you have no choice but to carry that shame. I should have accepted my guilt and left. Still, it's possible that ultimately a small amount of good came out of it, which I'll get to. I can only hope. And there was that scene in the hospital, of sitting with his dead mother, the promise that I would look after him.

As for my mother, to this day I've never been sure whether it was true she was mentally ill, but the idea sank into me like a drug, a poison, hidden under the surface, something I hardly processed, because soon after this scene of revelation and mania, when I was reborn "all pink and new," I used up my insurance policy's annual limit on visits, and therapy abruptly stopped.

CHAPTER TEN

Seven months later, winter came with holiday travel. I drove to Ohio and Indiana alone to see my parents, unable to sleep over the journey. Years later I realized it was my first time seeing my mother since being told she had a personality disorder. The stress of that, like so much else, got buried deep.

With no sleep night after night, in the mirror my distorted face looked back at me, stretched wide, eyes slanted and hollow. Losing the resemblance to my mother, I felt my father's face taking over the image, and I thought, *her face has lost her mother's bones*, and I muttered aloud, "My father will protect me." It was a strange thing, since I had never felt close to my father, but the revelation the previous summer about my mother had risen in me a new appreciation for him.

Mom talked about someone at her work being fired, and I wondered if she meant herself. Her bookshelves stuffed with Agatha Christie novels filled the air with murder, as did a crime show in the background on TV as a mother poisoned her son. Mom had always wanted to write a murder mystery. I felt she wanted to kill someone. She made deviled eggs, and I thought the pickle relish could disguise the taste of poison. She said, "I've been having terrible nightmares about pushing people into ovens."

From Ohio I drove to my father's house in Indiana. Still no sleep, exhausted to the bone. My father had remarried a woman whose family was nearby, so there were various adults and grandchildren in the house, a lot of food: ham, salads, etc.

My mom, who lived alone, had little food. She had orange marmalade waiting for me, as she knew I loved it, and there were the deviled eggs, and not much else. Much later when I talked it all over with my therapist, she said, "With your mother, you felt indulged, but with your father, you felt taken care of."

Well, that's cute and aphoristic, but the reality was my dad had a big household of people to feed, and my mom didn't. So I don't know if that was really a fair assessment.

As soon as I returned home, I had to go right back

on the road the next morning, to New Hampshire for a funeral. An elderly relative of my husband's had died. I spent another sleepless night before we left. It seems strange now that I had to go, and didn't stay home after my long drive. My husband could certainly have gone on his own, yet we never considered that.

Over that sleepless night, some terrible delusions began. I thought my mother had pushed her brother out of the car that day in 1949. In the morning, I left my mom a voicemail. "You are forgiven. You are forgiven. You can get help. You'll know a therapist is good if she tolerates silences. You are forgiven." A minute later, I thought, "I'm delusional," and I left another message, "Never mind. I don't know." And somehow I sounded normal enough in the second message, as she told me later, that she wasn't worried. My husband was nearby and didn't say a word.

I didn't want to ask the neighbors to watch our two cats, because we had recently asked them to for a different trip. I insisted we just take the cats with us to Nana's. I thought she wouldn't mind because she'd had cats in the past. My husband gave in. With my husband at the wheel, the cats at our feet in the front with us, I quickly regretted this absurd idea. He kept lowering his head to reach down to pet a cat. It all went into slow motion, his eyes off the road, his hands off the wheel. We didn't crash, but I cried out several times for him to watch the road.

At Nana's house, I was surprised she seemed annoyed about the cats, which we had to put in the basement. Gathered at Nana's were my husband's sister, eldest brother, and father. I don't remember if anyone else was there.

During the drive I'd had that sense of everything shifting to slow motion when my husband was reaching for the cats, and I wondered if that was a hallucination. That made me wonder how much I might have been hallucinating, and for how long? I was still well enough to do some reality testing.

Right after we arrived, I asked him, "You know how I've been hallucinating lately?" It was a funny way for me to put it. I already decided I must have been hallucinating.

There was a slight pause. His face lit up with a flicker of some positive feeling. He didn't ask me what on earth I was talking about. He simply said, "Yes."

I then asked him about a strange secret someone in the family had confided to him, which he'd told me a year or two earlier. I asked if it was real or if I had hallucinated it. I guess I asked about it because it was so strange, so it seemed like it might not be real. He confirmed it was real, and repeated it more loudly. Nana was nearby. I was startled that he repeated it so audibly, and hoped she didn't hear. He had no sense of privacy or confidentiality, and was opposed to people being "secretive." He was the last person you'd want to confide in.

His sister came up to me and said she wanted to show me something. She said it was something about Hannah Duston, that ancestor whose statue we had once visited. She held up a sheet of paper with some kind of weird, childish scrawl on it. Her father was sitting on a chair behind her, looking up at us, studying me with a knowing look on his face, as if he were awaiting a reaction from me. They seemed to have some plan. Not sleeping for eight nights had wiped out my ability to read, but whatever it was, it seemed weird and I sensed she was trying to rattle me in some way. I told her I hadn't slept in days and was unable to read.

A little later, sitting on the sofa with my husband, I said, "If I've really been a terrible wife all these years, you have permission to kill me." Without a word, he pulled me close in a big happy kiss, as if it was the nicest thing anyone had ever said to him.

The next morning, I started spouting delusions that my mother had repeatedly tried to kill me as a child, and that I was starting to remember. This is when their anger took its bizarre turn. Were they frightened? Shocked? Not at all.

Over breakfast while eating cereal I made the wild claim, repeating, "I'm remembering that my mother tried to kill me all the time when I was growing up."

No one was surprised. Their father sighed in mild exasperation. My sister-in-law responded, in a voice sharp with anger, "Feed the hungry child within you."

I was stunned. I felt her hatred, but I also was impressed, because I felt she was working hard to control her anger. I grabbed her hand and said, "You should be a minister!"

She got up to wash the breakfast dishes and replied that she would have been interested in ministry, but her atheist husband would never support it. I had no idea; it was a flash of insight for me to see it.

It was the day of the funeral for this elderly relative, the reason we had come. That morning as their older brother walked by me in the dining room, struggling with his necktie for the service, he said, "What drives me," he looked straight me, "*Nuts*, is..." I forget the rest. His point was clear. My psychosis was not an urgent medical emergency, merely an annoyance.

It probably seems from this story like I had been acting crazy around them for years, as if they didn't respond to my psychosis because they were used to it, but they had never witnessed mania from me before. Their nonchalance at my delusions was baffling, and added to my paranoia.

After the service, as day folded into night, it was abundantly clear something was very wrong with me. This was an emergency. They seemed pleased by it. Their response was to gather around the piano to sing church hymns.

On the wall, a photograph of their late grandfather, white-haired, grimacing, stared down at me with the face of the leader of a Satanic cult. Things fell into slow motion again. As they sang, shoulder to shoulder, their backs turned to me, it was as if they were celebrating that I was becoming psychotic. I wondered if my altered sense of reality was because they had poisoned me, that they were trying to drive me into psychosis, and now they were celebrating because they were succeeding.

I ran out into the snowy night, on legs like rubber. It seemed to take a long time for my husband to come after me and bring me back inside.

I ran up the stairs, calling "Nana, forgive me, forgive me!" On the side of the staircase were a hammer and some books. Chasing after me, my husband hit me on the back of the head with a blunt object. The blow wasn't hard, but I collapsed on the stairs to submit. When I asked him about it later he pretended I fell and hit my head on the stair, and said that he was afraid I was going to attack and kill Nana. He did hit me; he must have been trying to knock me unconscious so I wouldn't attack Nana. I hadn't threatened her at all. Perhaps my calling out, "forgive me" was something he took as a threat.

I thought they were poisoning me, they were Satanists, and they were all going to gather round to kill me and cut me apart with knives that night.

Lying in my husband's arms in bed that night, waiting in terror, he stroked my hair trying to lull me to sleep, and said in a cooing voice, "See the swans. How many swans are there?" In London, we spent time in Hyde Park surrounded by swans and ducks.

After he'd taken a lot of pictures of me feeding the ducks, he wanted one of himself feeding a swan. When he posed with the swan, I found he'd used up the film and no shots were left. He was deeply disappointed. I felt terribly guilty he didn't get his shot because he'd taken so many of me, and he made a point of telling me several times, even long afterward, how disappointing this was, not to get a picture feeding a swan. As he stroked my hair, repeating "See the swans. How many swans are there?" his voice softened and oozed into the sound of my mother's voice. Guilt overwhelmed me.

Early in the morning, before dawn, he made the decision. This couldn't go on. He drove me quickly in the dark, pointing at the H hospital signs we passed, calling, "Hospital! We're going to the hospital!" to keep me oriented. I was glad and excited, because he was rescuing me from the people who were going to kill me.

A man in a small room wrote a lot of notes on a computer; I don't remember there being many questions, yet he seemed to be typing for a long time. My husband's father joined us, coming separately, and we sat in the dark little office while the man wrote. My father-in-law talked about waking from a dream in which he'd been wandering outside a factory looking for a bathroom. My husband said he'd have to call his work to get extra time off. Still a delivery man, he worked for Airborne Express. He repeated the number he'd have to call, "1-800-*Air Born*," several times, stressing the company name in a weird way as if it had special meaning.

I was alone with the man who was taking the notes. I briefly touched his knee as he sat next to me, telling him something of how I felt, I forget what, and I could see he was flattered that I shared this moment of closeness with him. But I immediately drew back, thinking I should not have shown this intimacy, and said something rejecting, that I was too personal with men sometimes, and his face fell because I had withdrawn the compliment.

A nurse rode with my husband and me up the elevator to the fifth-floor psych ward. New and plush, the niceness was disorienting, like heaven's waiting room.

We met with a nurse and a psychiatrist, whom I never saw again, and I accused myself of all kinds of crazy things I hadn't done, and I said something or other about God. The psychiatrist asked if I'd like to try some Klonopin. The nurse flashed him a look of disapproval, at least, it seemed to me.

Another nurse and my husband sat down with me in the common area and I was offered a pill to take to sleep. I thought a prescription always had to be in a labeled bottle to be legal, so the pill just sitting next to the glass of water seemed illegal and confusing.

What I feared was not merely dying. What I felt was I had done many terrible things in my life, and if I died, I would never have the opportunity to make up for it all.

I finally took the pill. They walked me to my bedroom. My husband said at the doorway, "You're just going to *sleep*!" This frightened me again and I ran to the bathroom and threw up the pill. I wish I could tell the nurse now I'm sorry. I understand how frustrated she was. She came back with a needle. The shot was like a punch in the arm, and my last thought was, "I wouldn't have tried to grab it from you," because I thought that was probably why she was so assertive about it. As I passed out on the bed, the eyes in my husband's satisfied face looked odd and naked, since he'd recently begun the habit of pulling out his eyelashes.

CHAPTER ELEVEN

I slept all day. My memory of this chronology is a bit fuzzy, because I know I missed dinner that night. But I got up around sunset. That evening in the ward, I feared my phone message to my mom had driven her to suicide. Patients were allowed to use a pay phone. I had a calling card in my wallet, a prepaid card we used in the old days. I called her local police department in Columbus, Ohio, and reported I was afraid my mom had committed suicide. My oldest brother was a police officer in Columbus at the time, and he told me later they reached out to him to ask if his mom was okay, and everything was fine.

After I called the police, I stared out the big window of the ward's living room on the fifth floor, gazing at the purple clouds of sunset, thinking my mom's soul was rising to heaven. A few yards away, a woman was staring at me. I was later introduced to her as the art therapist. It was clear she was watching me, fascinated, perhaps thinking to herself, "What is this mad woman thinking about? What delusions is she having?" Yes, I was having a delusion, but I could also see this woman staring and thinking about it, and it irritated me very much.

I think I might have gone back to bed then; that must be why I missed dinner. When I woke again, a nurse brought me out of my room and you had just arrived in the hallway by the nurse's counter, nine o'clock on a Sunday night. You were still in your tan bomber jacket, not having entered your office yet. I felt foolish for having been so crazy.

Because I had finally slept, I was already somewhat better. "Hi," I said with a big smile, a smile that was meant to say, "I know I've been crazy. I'm embarrassed."

You said, "Hi," with a small, shy smile, and I thought your smile was cute.

Once you were settled in your office, I came in and we sat on two small, lightweight, white chairs at one end of the room, facing each other, your desk at the other end in front of the window. You held a clipboard to take notes. You asked the date, and after everything that had happened, after having been passed out all day, I knew the date: January 3, 1993. Unlike my childhood nightmare, I knew what day it was.

You asked who the president was—Clinton was going to be inaugurated in a couple of weeks—and you asked how many fingers you were holding up. Four.

You interviewed me and I described how I drove all that way by myself before having to get back on the road to New Hampshire. I traced a map of the trip to Ohio and Indiana in the air with my index finger. I felt like this charmed you.

You asked about the funeral I was in town for, and I assured you that there was no trauma around this distant relative's death, since I quickly understood you were concerned about that. And I cried, telling you how guilty I felt for being such a terrible wife for seven years. You handed me a box of tissues from the desk.

You were wearing a gray polo shirt, gray pants, and gray suede shoes. I thought suede shoes were a risky choice for winter, wondering if they might get stained with salt. Your wedding ring looked especially thick on your hand, unmissable. Glasses magnified your brown eyes. Over the years since, I learned that you were thirty-eight years old, and that you'd been in charge of the psych ward for four years. You must have come from home on your night off, that late Sunday evening. After that night, you wore suits, lovely wool suits, double breasted; you seemed so tall in that brown suit with its gold buttons, and I always felt such a strong attraction to a man in a suit.

Your office was extremely neat and bare, not a single stray paper on your desk. It was such a contrast to the messy office of the ward I was in later, the one you sent me to in handcuffs. There were two watercolors on the wall behind you, and I thought they were either by a patient or your child. I decided they were by your child.

You ordered Trilafon for me, an antipsychotic, to take that night. After you left, I refused it. I was terrified of taking it. I also felt, now that I'd slept, that I was no longer psychotic, because I knew what was real.

The next morning when you came in and discovered I'd refused the medication, I was in my room, and you arrived in a rush with two female nurses in tow. The team was meant to convince me to take the drug. I said I was remembering childhood abuse and wanted to talk about it. You said taking the medication would be "efficient." An unfortunate choice of word. During my bouts of mania, I had this moral opposition to efficiency. I felt speed and efficiency were terrible things in this world.

Still weak and exhausted, my voice a low, tremulous moan, I said, "I'm *sure* I was taking my lithium, I'm *sure* of it. Maybe I hallucinated taking it."

Later I read the note of that in your report. Yet I hadn't hallucinated it. I counted the pills in the bottle afterward and the number left indicated I actually never skipped a dose through all of this.

It was strange, though. This one nurse came to me after that conversation, and I had such a strong sensation she was pleased I had argued with you, she was so smiley, almost giddy. I decided there was some conflict here, that maybe she was glad I'd resisted you. Was she? Why did she seem so happy?

At this point, I thought it strange that they let me place this call to the police the night before. Surely they must have overheard me. It hit me: they had no idea I had a calling card. They didn't know it was a real call. They thought I was just play-acting on the phone.

Across from the nurse's station was a very dark office, where a man was typing. I had this odd sensation he was typing transcripts of our phone conversations. I told him that I had called the police in Columbus the night before.

"Yes?" he said jovially.

Clearly he didn't know. "I have a calling card," I said.

His jaw dropped. "You have a calling card?"

"Yes."

I left him to his typing. The nurse who had seemed so giddy hurried up to me a few minutes later to ask about the call, and I told her about it. She took it in without comment. And I have to say, I was really disappointed that no one thanked me or praised me for having the presence of mind to let you guys know this.

That morning, we met again, and I reported to you I had a dissociative disorder "on top of" my bipolar disorder, according to my therapist. I wonder what you made of that. Many years later, a questionnaire from a therapist established that I did not have a dissociative disorder at all: I never found myself places without knowing how I got there, or forgot buying things, or any of that. In the evaluation I asked for and read many years later, you mentioned the dissociative disorder as "reported," making clear this was from me and not necessarily your diagnosis.

While I slept the previous day, my husband had brought some clothes for me. For some reason, a pair of his underwear was among them. I assumed it was an oversight on his part. I found it eerie.

A nurse gave me a tour of the ward. In the kitchenette I noticed right away someone had dumped coffee grounds on top of the soda cans in the recycling. There were a lot of grounds as if this had been going in for a while and no one had noticed. There was a living area with a TV, but no one really watched TV the whole time I was there, except for one movie night. The main pastime among the other patients was doing jigsaw puzzles. There weren't many patients; a couple of young women trying out antidepressants, a middle-aged man, and an elderly woman who kept rubbing her nose, which I was also doing because it wouldn't stop itching.

I didn't like the artwork in your ward. My room had a print of bunnies on it, and I felt their eyes were judging me. In the hall was a Cubist print of a subway station that looked to me like someone being crushed in a revolving door.

My husband visited as I ate breakfast in the dining area by the kitchenette. I said to him, "I know I've been a terrible wife to you for seven years. I promise to stay seven more years and make it up to you."

He replied in a ghoulish voice, "Seven *times* seven."

After a good night's sleep, I was doing better, and I wished the nurses were observing me more to see how much saner I was. Once as I chatted with the two young women, they had the same complaint, that the nurses didn't seem to want to interact with us; one said they were "hiding in their offices."

It was true I still thought my mother had tried to kill me, but otherwise I was interacting normally with people. One evening the old woman was stuck trying to open the door of the laundry room with an armful of clothes. I was the only one who noticed. I helped her through the door, wishing again the nurses were noticing me.

The first morning, after you and the nurses tried to get me to take the Trilafon, my twin brother called the ward. My husband had let the family know what happened, and my brother had called the hospital only to be told I'd been discharged, and all was confusion. The hospital had finally put him through to the nurse's station, and when one handed me the phone, you and a nurse sat on the opposite side of the counter. As I talked to my brother, I could tell the two of you were repeating my words to each other to listen in on my conversation.

I broke in and interrupted you. You rolled your chair back a couple of feet with a glare at the nurse. I knew what this look meant. Your glare was to say, "She's onto us and this was *your* idea." But I only interrupted to ask if you knew why my brother had been told I'd been discharged. Your face fell regretfully, as you said you didn't know.

I knew all this, but it wasn't important. I had bigger fish to fry.

I insisted to you I wanted to talk about my mother trying to kill me as a child. But there was no reason to. I understand that now. Without getting the psychosis under control with some meds, I would have just continued to spout those delusions.

The second night, we made a community supper supervised by a nurse and the art therapist. We made subs, which they referred to in the New England way as "grinders," and I sliced peppers with a young man who'd been admitted that day. There were literally half a dozen sharp knives laid out in front of us. No one would think that would happen in a psych ward, would they? But yes, we had a bunch of sharp knives right there. As we sliced the peppers, the young man said to me, his face growing red, "Do you know why I'm here? Because I'm so angry I'm a danger to myself and others!" The staff had no idea he was saying this to me as he plunged the knife into the peppers. It made me nervous, but even then I thought it was hilarious.

The next day, I told you I felt unsafe that he was allowed to handle knives. "What?" you asked in shock. The truth is, this was spiteful of me. That art therapist, who was in charge of our dinner, had irritated me, first by staring at me the first night, and in other ways, and especially that she paid no attention while this guy said these dangerous things to me, so I enjoyed the possibility this would get her in a little bit of trouble.

At our dinner of grinders that night, the staff observed us without participating in the conversation as we all chitchatted quite normally. We all noticed our plastic ID wrist bands were different colors. Mine was white; others were pink or green. We wondered if there was any reason for this, whether it reflected our diagnosis or meant anything. Just something we were curious about.

During my final talk with you, I asked you about it. Years later when I read your evaluation, I was shocked to see in your report that I was "obsessed" with the wrist bands and thought they had "magical properties." Sheesh, I was only idly curious! Yes, I was crazy, but I wasn't *that* crazy. Come on!

Your report also mentioned that my husband blew up at a nurse because he wasn't allowed to spend nights with me at the ward. I guess that was why he had added his underwear to my clothes.

I was there three days, and don't recall much more of my interaction with you, but it seemed like on the middle day, you just sat there looking at your clipboard during our meeting, as if waiting for me to spontaneously say something. I do remember one moment. I said something to you about my concern a nurse was mad at me. You said, "I think you're reading too much into it." That really struck me and I was very grateful for that moment of honesty. I was raised in a dishonest house, and that simple response was so *authentic*. You didn't say it in a judgy way—just the opposite. You said it as if you trusted me to accept it, as if you saw me as intelligent and discerning. As if we were equals. That meant so much. It meant everything.

We were at a stalemate, because I still refused to take the Trilafon, and my husband had to get back home, back to his job. On the third day, I decided to leave. It wasn't a locked ward; I was there voluntarily. My husband joined us for the final interview. I was getting slightly better from having been able to sleep, but the previous night you hadn't ordered Ativan, so after another restless night, I was drifting in and out of lucidity. I said, "It's hard to trust." And you snapped impatiently, "I just said that, Amy!" I felt you were angry and wanted me to leave. Only later did I understand you were simply frustrated. You were probably tired, too. I know now you would have had a toddler and either a baby or a pregnant wife at home.

Rather than state a diagnosis, you said several times that I had "a physical problem causing dissociation."

Suddenly it hit me you were avoiding something, avoiding giving it a label. I asked, "Does it have a *name*?"

You drew in your breath, as if this were an unexpected question and you saw I had noticed your avoidance. But you merely repeated the same words. As if you were hiding something. You said something to the effect that I might not be properly diagnosed because I was "so verbal." Something was going on here.

Even now, what I think is: you suspected I might be a misdiagnosed schizophrenic. But you couldn't say so, not so soon. Your hands were tied. It's a big deal to change a diagnosis, especially to something as damning as schizophrenia. It can't be done lightly. I think that might even be why you wrote that exaggeration in my evaluation, about the wrist bands' "magical properties." Maybe you were trying to establish how psychotic I was to lay the groundwork for a future change in my diagnosis.

I also wondered later what communication you had with my therapist back in New York, if you had argued. Maybe you suggested to her I was misdiagnosed, and she was adamant you were wrong. I wonder this because when it came up that I had stopped seeing her, I'd forgotten the reason was the insurance limit. I told you it was because she'd finished her residency. It was true she was finishing her residency, but it wasn't the reason we'd stopped.

Your face lit up with surprise and displeasure. "She's only a *resident*?" you asked.

But that last morning my sense you were hiding something made another roadblock between us.

I said, "You know me *so well*, after three days."

And you said, "Yes, Amy, I *do*," with a firm nod of the head. As I said before, this came out delightfully flirtatious. Now, I do understand you might have been only mirroring my own tone, but it was still a lovely moment.

You were wearing the necktie with scientific formulas on it. My husband turned to you and said, "I *like* your tie." A pause. You said, "Thank you."

I thought, here I am in this serious situation, and these men only care about their neckties. I extended my annoyance toward both of you. But I can see your face now, how stiffly and coldly you said, "Thank you."

At one point, I reached for your hand, and you took mine, and I felt like I was a little old lady, and this nice young man was holding my hand. Drifting in and out, I had a sense of being submerged under water, unable to speak.

And then you gave up, slapping your hands against your knees with a gesture of finality. If we had talked five more minutes, would I have stayed? But my husband wanted me to leave. He was furious with that nurse, and wanted to take me home. With your moment of frustration that seemed a little angry, it felt like you wanted me to leave, too, and that I wasn't allowed to stay if I wouldn't take your medication.

I stood up and pulled out the pair of scissors from the pen container on your desk and leaned toward you, holding out my wrist for you to cut off the plastic ID. You gave a start. I thought you were flustered by this obvious romantic gesture. Later I wondered if your fluster was because you thought I was going to attack you with the scissors. Composing yourself, you said the nurse could cut off the band.

You asked which brand of lithium I took, Lithonate or Eskalith. I told you Lithonate. When I left, I saw you'd written the prescription for Eskalith instead. Did you do that on purpose so I'd come back? Or am I reading too much into it? I didn't come back for you to fix it, only filled the Eskalith since it wasn't an important difference.

In my room, a nurse went over a checklist with me for my exit, making sure I'd left nothing behind, etc. A year or two earlier, I'd begun to think something was wrong with my husband. While my illness had caused that concern to fall by the wayside, I hadn't completely forgotten, and I said to the nurse, "I don't know what's wrong with my husband, but we'll deal with it."

I shook your hand at the doorway. We left. A nurse joined us to go down the elevator. She said, "You can always write to us."

Did you curse her later for saying this? Did you expect to get letters from me for thirty years?

CHAPTER TWELVE

We went back to Nana's, and immediately I scrawled a letter to you. Since I was sure you were hiding something from me, I thought it must be that I was dying, that I had Alzheimer's. Why else would you refuse to say? I sent you a note saying I figured it out, and put the letter in Nana's mailbox and put the flag up.

Before heading back to New York, my husband and I went for a walk in a park. It wasn't cold that January day, and the sun shone on the evergreen trees and thin layer of snow. We had the park to ourselves. I wasn't fully recovered, but bit by bit, I was getting better. Mania isn't a permanent thing; it does wear off. I was enough better that I wanted to sort things out and reason through what had happened, to look objectively at my delusions of that week.

I said to my husband, "The reason I thought I was being poisoned was because food tasted metallic to me."

I was about to say, maybe the iron in the raisins could have tasted metallic, when without missing a beat, he said, "Arsenic's a metal, isn't it?"

I wasn't well enough to cope with that response. My mind raced, thinking he was confessing. As soon as we got back to Nana's, I called for an ambulance, claiming I had been poisoned. At the hospital emergency room, I said I would take any medication they required if they would just please test me for arsenic.

I ended up alone again with the man who'd done the first intake, the man whom I felt I had flattered by touching his knee. This time I reached for his hand and said, "I'm not going to take back the compliment this time," and I could see this pleased him, that he hadn't forgotten that exchange from before. I'm glad I had the chance to do that.

But it turned out, the hospital policy was that a patient who left the psych ward against medical advice could not be re-admitted. My husband arrived, and the policeman on duty asked if I wanted to go home with my husband. I said no. Officially involuntarily committed, I was taken in handcuffs by the police to the locked state ward in Manchester. I never saw you, and I'll never know if you knew I had come back that day. Was it your decision not to let me back, did you reject me? or was it only an automatic policy by the hospital which was out of your hands?

The handcuffs and ride in the police car didn't upset me. They were keeping me safe from my husband poisoning me.

I liked the artwork in the state ward better: pretty still lives with flower bouquets. In that ward, I shared a bedroom with a roommate. I taught her to play chess. There was a lot of chess playing in the state ward.

I demanded to be tested for arsenic, promising again to take any medication they advised in exchange. They drew blood, and the doctor reported I actually had less than the normal level of arsenic. (Is there really a normal level for arsenic?) For medication they gave me Navane.

I don't know if there was any communication between you and the psychiatrist in the state ward. He was a big bear of a man, who didn't wear suits, just button-down shirts, and black pants. His small, dark office was a mess, his desk covered with stacks of papers, books, and files.

The nurses at the state ward were more casual and friendly than in yours. They played chess with us. After they did my blood work, a full work-up, and it came up that I thought people were going to kill me, a male nurse joked, "I'd kill for your cholesterol level." It turned out my cholesterol was only 120. We had a nice laugh over it.

The nurses in your ward were quite well dressed, I thought almost overdressed. I recall a slim young nurse in a tight, cream-colored sweater dress. I thought it was rather sexy for a psych ward. The nurses in the state ward wore jeans.

When you wanted me to take the Trilafon, I had heard it as Trilo-phan, and thought it might be related to L-Tryptophan. I wanted to comply now, wanted to do the right thing, so in case they were related, I kept drinking little cartons of milk from the ward's refrigerator.

My husband went home, to return for me when I was released. During the week, he talked on the phone with the psychiatrist. I don't know what they discussed, but before I left, the psychiatrist said, "Your husband asked if you'd be coming home in a pine box. Should I be concerned about that?" I was confused, and only realized later that the psychiatrist was wondering if I'd expressed suicidal thoughts to my husband. I don't remember speaking to my husband at all while I was there. I don't think I did.

I was released from Manchester after only a week. I don't know why they let me go so soon. I assumed I must be all better. I think it's possible my husband had promised them he would admit me to a local ward when we got home, but he didn't. There had been news stories while I was away about a couple of patients who died in a local psych ward. That must be why he had brought up the pine box on the phone to the doctor, and maybe why he decided not to admit me once we were home.

CHAPTER THIRTEEN

Since this was January, a new year, my insurance would let me see a therapist again at last. I went back to the one I'd been seeing, the one who'd diagnosed my mother with a personality disorder. When I told her about my hospitalization and about you, she immediately said, with a touch of humor and disdain, "Sometimes there are bad psychiatrists."

Wow. She was in for a shock when it was clear I'd fallen in love with you.

Her negative comment encouraged my suspicion that you did want to diagnose me as schizophrenic, the two of you had talked on the phone and disagreed, maybe she even forbade you to take such a damning step. I wonder whether you asked her to convince me to take the Trilafon. If she had told me to take it, I certainly would have.

After we got home, my husband said what I

had suffered was "sleep deprivation psychosis." Not knowing he had picked this up from an episode of the TV show *M*A*S*H*, I wrote to you about this amateur diagnosis.

The next week my therapist started off the session by saying there was no such thing as sleep deprivation psychosis. I hadn't mentioned this to her. Clearly you were sharing my letters, though she never said so. It was obvious my writing to you irritated her. I confessed to her I was writing you letters and how guilty I felt about it. Once when I mentioned something, I forget what, she said, dripping with sarcasm, "Why don't you write him a letter about it?" This hurt a lot. I couldn't believe she'd be sarcastic about something I felt such guilt over. It was pretty passive-aggressive of her. I didn't react, didn't tell her how this cut me to the quick.

You let me talk on the phone with you, just once, a few weeks after I got home. I called the ward and the nurse said excitedly, "He wants to talk with you." It was wonderful to hear that. You asked, "How are you?" with so much care in your soft voice. It felt like you were the only person in my life who was worried about me. We only spoke briefly. I forgot to ask if you thought I was schizophrenic. I don't remember much of the conversation, except that you said more than once to be sure not to hide any of my symptoms from my therapist. This again supports my theory. I told you I wasn't.

Several times I wrote you, saying, "Don't worry about me," but I did want you to be. I wanted someone to be.

It wasn't until after this that I felt I'd fallen in love with you. I'd been writing to you for several months, and I had a dream. We were sitting on a sofa, or perhaps it was a bed. I asked you if you had a long commute to the hospital, and you said you did. I said I thought you probably had a big car, and we were laughing about this big car, and we kissed. In the soft, impalpable dream it was the Platonic ideal of a kiss, with the dreaminess of incorporeality and the reality of dream logic. I awoke realizing I loved you, had loved you all along.

I read about bipolar disorder, and the symptoms didn't seem to fit. I read about schizophrenia, and it seemed a better description, even in odd little ways, like the fact that during that episode I had an inexplicable, psychosomatic cough. It also seemed to explain some of the veiled things you said to me. I started to insist to my therapist that I be treated for schizophrenia.

I was certain of one thing: lithium wasn't doing a thing. I had been taking every dose like I was supposed to, and it had no effect at all. I tried to get them to put me on an antipsychotic. I'll never know why they refused, except that an assumption was made that my episode was due to noncompliance about the lithium, a biased assumption professionals make about people like me. In your report, you too had assumed that I was noncompliant, because my lithium blood level was 0.5 when I was admitted. No one knew my psychiatrist had expressed those earlier doubts about my diagnosis and had kept my blood level that low on purpose. I didn't know at the time that everyone's assumption was merely that I was noncompliant, so I never had the chance to explain. By then three years had gone by since that psychiatrist had made the decision to keep my lithium blood level low, and even she might have forgotten.

At one point that spring after I was hospitalized, the psychiatrist surprised me by telling me to take my lithium all at once rather than spread it out over the day. Supposedly some new research suggested this, but lithium is never prescribed that way. Usually you take three little capsules a day. A year or two later, I asked my next psychiatrist about her advice to take them all at once. He replied, "Well, she's been hitting the bottle pretty hard lately. She was probably under the influence when she said that." He actually didn't say "she's," he referred to her by her first name. It was a bit of a shock.

I realized, yes, she was odd sometimes. Like one time when she suddenly laughed in a weird way. She was drunk.

That spring, though, she still intimidated me, and she was my therapist's boss. I asked my therapist if I could talk to this psychiatrist about changing my medication. With a snort, she replied, "I'd like to be a fly on the wall for *that* conversation." I was stunned. It was the exact thing to say to make sure I wouldn't ever try to bring it up to her.

But I did still want a change. Hoping to force them to prescribe something else, I finally stopped taking the lithium. This was the only time I was noncompliant about it. I thought if I refused it, they would give in and prescribe something more effective, like I wanted. It never got through to them that was my goal, because I demanded to be treated for schizophrenia, and my therapist was adamant I wasn't schizophrenic. This distracted everyone from what should have been the obvious need to change my medication.

I even demanded they give me an MRI at one point. I felt my psychosis had enough physical symptoms that maybe I had a brain tumor. For example, at one point in New Hampshire I felt the room grow dark and that we were sitting in a small pool of light. I knew they'd have the results that Monday. They didn't call me. I thought, okay, I'm dying. I burned a lot of old stories and letters in our wood stove. I figured my therapist was waiting until our Thursday appointment to let me know in person I was dying. Thursday came. I was fine. They just didn't bother to let me know on Monday when I knew they had the results of the MRI. I didn't tell her anything about how they let me think I was dying and I burned all those papers.

All that spring after that hospitalization, I wasn't well. My fear of going insane included the terrible fear of losing control of myself. One night my husband and I watched a TV movie about Ted Bundy, the serial killer. When we went to bed, I told him I was afraid I might kill him, that I would be sort of hypnotized by this film. I was just so scared of losing my grip on reality.

My husband was really wonderful to me in that moment. He put his arms around me and assured me I was okay, that everything was okay. It was a really precious moment for me in all those years.

When I told my therapist the next day, at first I couldn't remember the name of the actor who played Bundy. She got hung up on trying to remember. When I told her of my awful fear, and that I'd told it to my husband, she laughed. She thought it was funny and wondered if my husband slept that night. In the middle of my telling her this, she broke in with the name of the actor, Mark Harmon, which popped into her head.

She laughed at what was my greatest fear. I wanted to punch her.

I was drifting in and out of manic delusions that spring, which lithium or no lithium didn't affect. One thing that worried me was the weather. I said to the therapist, "I'm having a delusion about the weather. Not exactly that I'm in control of the weather. But that the weather is a response to my actions. Like, if I'm thinking of sending someone a letter, and it starts raining, that means I should send the letter, so I send it."

The therapist said with casual confidence, "If you know it's a delusion, it's not a delusion." And she dropped the subject. I should have found a new set of doctors then and there.

In terms of this particular delusion, I had a revelation about it decades later. After I was given the right medication, I rarely became manic again. But I did have a breakout episode long after. I recently tried writing a one-woman show about it, a monologue. I'm going to paste here the description of how it felt.

You are walking, and the universe is speaking to you. The angels watching over you send their messages. You're thinking of something you want to say to him, and someone walking by on his cell phone says, "Smothering," and it's a sign not to smother him. A hawk glides across the sky, a sign. A snatch of music, a sign. Everything a sign. There's so much you know.

Your hearing is extra sensitive. A loud voice makes you cringe in pain. Faces reveal so much, it's like you can read their minds.

You breathe hard, exhausted from not sleeping. You lie down. Your body is glowing, phosphorescent. You want only to be very still, falling inside yourself. You can hardly speak.

You don't want to speak or hear anyone. You lie still, pulsing and glowing, tapping into a thread of the universe, your breath like the sound effect of from 2001: a Space Odyssey, the heavy breathing in a space suit. You are drowning in the air, pulsing and glowing.

Your husband is worried. He comes in and lies next to you, his arm around you. My God please, go away. I don't want you here. I don't want your worry. I don't want your body so close, I don't want to be touched. I don't want to talk. But you know he's worried, you can't say it, you can't hurt his feelings. You want only to fall and keep falling, falling into the universe, glowing and pulsing with the universe, phosphorescent.

It's time to go for a walk. You walk together. He is talking about a movie. You try to talk about the movie. You try to keep up. He tries to keep you in the world. There are signs. A bird is a sign, the slam of a car door, a sign. A street sign is a sign. He says something about the movie. You ask about the director. You wish you didn't have to talk, falling into yourself, drinking the signals of the universe. Everything a signal, everything a message from the universe.

You think about the man who died and if he is watching over you and a flock of pigeons fills the sky. Yes. Your husband is talking about Deadpool and you try to listen but you're listening to the dead. The dead who flit on the tree branches with flicker-

ing wings, the dead who guided the hand of the child drawing chalk numbers on the sidewalk: your lucky number 5, 5 pointed star, you're the fifth of five children, the dead who decided a cicada would shriek just when you think of something you want to write to someone, the cicada shrieking no no no. The dead who decided the name of the street, a name from your past life. And it's all filling your body with secret understanding and a well of silence pushing against the noise, a pool, a dead pool of silence consuming the noise, you swim in it, the air is thick with meaning, taut with tense pulsing desire. And you think you can know everything, because all is being uncovered.

And you're wondrous and afraid. Am I the Messiah? Am I enlightened? Is this enlightenment? Am I a Buddha? And you know there is no one Messiah, we are all messiahs, many messiahs. And you remember the time 30 years ago when you were walking by a dairy farm and a herd of huge cows jumped, leapt up and started chasing after you along the fence. Because you are electricity! You are threaded to the universe, glowing and pulsing, and you don't feel your feet while you walk.

And you're afraid you're the messiah, and what happened to the last messiah, and you're afraid you'll be crucified, you're afraid you'll be murdered, glowing and pulsing, and you're afraid you're enlightened, knowing all are enlightened, every moment enlightened, glowing and pulsing.

And you try to sleep and all you can do is think about that kiss, how you want that kiss, for once in my life, those kisses glowing and pulsing, for once in my life, your breath trembling on his cheek, your hand in his hair soft as moss, madly kissing, pulsing and glowing, madly kissing, your hand in his hair soft as moss.

And finally, finally, the chemicals drain. The tide turns. The storm runs out. The winds calm. And you walk in the park, and the bird is not a sign, the slam of the car door is not a sign, the street sign is not a sign.

And you think, thank God I'm bipolar. Thank God I'm only mentally ill. Because I am not enlightened, I am only bipolar. I am not the messiah, I am only bipolar. I am not a Buddha, I am only bipolar. Thank God I am not enlightened. I'm only bipolar. Thank God I am not the Messiah. I am only bipolar. Thank God I am not a Buddha. I am only bipolar. And it is a gift, an illness, yet a gift. It will protect me. It will always protect me, from anyone in the world who might think I am enlightened, that I am a messiah. Because now they can say, she's only bipolar. She has a mental illness. She was just cutting back on her meds. She is only bipolar. She is not a messiah. She is only bipolar.

And in the park, a bird is only a bird. A car door is only a car door. A street sign is only a street sign. And the mountain is a mountain again. The mountain is a mountain again. The mountain is only a mountain…

As I came out of this, I had a revelation, and it was the revelation I could have had with that therapist thirty years earlier. That that particular delusion of seeing signs everywhere is simply confirmation bias. That you see these signs of affirmation because you want the universe to say yes to your manic desires. That's basically it. Almost any psychologist would know this.

CHAPTER FOURTEEN

That summer, a suspicion started burrowing into my unconscious: there was something terribly wrong with my husband. I never told anyone these delusions, didn't make any wild accusations, thank God. As psychosis welled in me, I thought that my husband was mentally retarded, that everything he'd accomplished in his life was in spite of a terrible mental disability, that this had been hidden by his family, and I had been tricked into marrying him. One August night I thought that he had poisoned his mother, and his family had castrated him in punishment. Thank God I said none of this aloud. It was terrifying.

Night descended. I didn't scream or spout delusions. I barely spoke a word. I grabbed a kitchen knife to put out my eyes, silently looking at him to decide what I should do. The night was dark. There were no overhead lights in our house, and a single lamp cast a shadow over his expressionless, impassive face. Coy dogs loudly chattered a devilish language from the woods behind the house. Calmly, he took the knife from my hand.

He broke open a couple of Benadryl capsules and poured the granules onto a spoon for me to swallow. Years earlier I'd insisted that I only needed sleep to be well. To him it was the betrayal of a promise if sleep wasn't the answer. But his behavior was also a punishment. If it wasn't true that sleep was the answer, then I had lied to him, so he was bound to hold me to this claim to the last possible instant.

I swallowed the bitter granules. Again he waited until morning to hospitalize me. As I waited for them to take me to the ward, they had me lie down in a waiting room. My husband and this guy kept chatting as I lay there. I indicated this was bothering me. So they went into his office next door where they continued their stupid chatter. This bothered me, too. What I really wanted was for them to sit with me in silence.

Apparently my agitation, though I don't think it was pronounced, prompted them to decide I should be injected with Ativan. In the hall, a nurse made me lower my pants to be injected in the butt. This seemed rather gratuitous because it can certainly go in the arm just as well. But perhaps it was to make sure I didn't try to grab the needle.

Years later, I asked a psychiatrist how long it takes for Ativan to knock you out. He said about fifteen minutes. When they inject you, it feels immediate. You have no memory of anything after the moment the needle goes in.

I woke in a room in the psych ward. It was early and the morning shift was starting. I was in agony over the fact that I kept becoming psychotic. I quickly took off one of my shoelaces and wrapped it around my neck to try to kill myself. A nurse came in and took off the shoelace, and took the other one from my other shoe, calmly, gently, without any comment. I think maybe I was put on a 24-hour suicide watch that day, but it was all handled discreetly.

Lying in bed in that early morning, a voice from the hall said, "I'm a vampire." I didn't know that was slang for a phlebotomist. At that moment a male nurse came in to check on me, a bald man with pointy ears who did look vampiric. It was all eerie.

My psychiatrist, the fox-woman who intimidated me, who I was too afraid of even to ask to change my meds when I asked the therapist about it, visited me once and said with wonder, "When you go, you really go!"

I wanted to punch her and shout, "What do you think happened in January? Why did you refuse to take that seriously?"

At last I was put on an antipsychotic, Haldol, and recovered quickly, but I was disabled, thoroughly weakened, in a lifeless fog. My life seemed over. In a letter to a friend, I almost wrote "the future is bleak," but I didn't want to seem so despairing, and didn't finish the sentence. The phrase "the future is" I merely crossed out, and it was visible in the pentimento, as if my future had been canceled.

The Haldol made my face stiff and unable to emote. After a rare get-together with my family, my aunt, who was a doctor, told my mom she was worried about the fact that I wasn't blinking.

Funnily, I still worked as a substitute teacher that year. I had this weird problem—was it because of the medication?—that I couldn't get my hair to dry. I'd try skipping the conditioner, using a blow dryer, but nothing would get my hair to dry. They stopped calling me to teach after one of my wet-hair days.

After seven months on Haldol, in February of 1994, I was put on a drug new on the market, Risperdal, the brand name of risperidone. It was a miracle. That alcoholic psychiatrist made the decision that saved my life, because risperidone is so effective for me, that I've been almost symptom-free ever since. I may have a rare bout of hypomania, but nothing severe, only if triggered by stress, and these bouts have become more and more rare, years apart. The episode I described earlier was the only serious one I've had in over thirty years.

I know it's unusual to find such an effective treatment. I'm lucky, and grateful. I would not have been able to go on living if these frightening episodes were inevitable for the rest of my life. Without risperidone my fate would be a hellish nightmare of frequent psychosis, maybe an early death. As it became clear the medication worked so miraculously, I wrote to you, "Psychiatry is the science of overcoming fate." Were you touched by that?

Yet I still wondered for a long time if I were a misdiagnosed schizophrenic. Years later, settled in Chicago and living a normal life, I googled bipolar disorder and stumbled upon a reference to "bipolar disorder with psychotic features." That was it!

I wrote this to you, then screwed up my nerve and wrote to your ward, demanding to be sent your evaluation of my time there. I had to know if you thought I was misdiagnosed. The evaluation arrived in the mail. Your form said bipolar disorder, then there was a gap on the page, then "with psychotic features." As if you'd added that later, upon receiving my letter. It also said, "endogamous obesity," then a gap, then "mild." Thanks for adding "mild." I wrote back to you joking you forgot to mention my adult acne. By then I had a new life, and getting this accurate diagnosis buoyed my fresh start.

CHAPTER FIFTEEN

There were aspects of our house that were starting to fall apart. Twice we were hit with a wind vortex that might have qualified as a tornado sweeping up the valley. It twisted the metal chimney of our woodstove so it needed to be replaced. My husband took the woodstove out and threw it in the yard. Under it, we'd had a metal pad that was made to go under woodstoves, but we found under the pad the plywood floor was slightly charred, so we also needed to pour some concrete instead of using this pad. Neither got done. My husband's brother-in-law was disappointed at the sight of the woodstove sitting out in the grass, the gift from his late father.

Our gas oven, which had a built-in-heater, failed. The man delivering propane looked at it and said it needed a raster valve. It was never fixed and I no longer had an oven. To take care of the heat, my husband installed electric baseboards.

We had a big riding mower for the two-acre field around our house, which his father gave us when we moved in since he had gotten himself a new one. One day, my husband tried filling it with gas while the engine was running, causing it to burst into flames. That was it for ever mowing the lawn again. After that, in summer we had to precariously dodge the webs filled with black and green garden spiders throughout the wildflower lawn.

As I got better, my husband and I tried seeing a marriage counselor for a few sessions. She asked me to say how I felt when he talked about his invention and going into outer space. With unexpected emotion, a catch in my voice, I said, "I feel *lonely* when you talk about going into space." The next week my husband said, "Last week, when you said my invention was *stupid...*" That was what he heard.

My ex-husband's belief in his invention, that he knew the secret of a generator that would produce more energy than it consumed, led to other beliefs. Of course, the oil companies and government would want to prevent his invention. Sometimes the phone would ring and there'd be no one on the other end, which was becoming common with the new world of computer-automated sales calls. But he thought there was something suspicious about it, that our phone was tapped.

This built up to the point that one day at a party in 1996, I overheard him say that our new neighbor was a government agent spying on us. My hair almost stood on end. That was the tipping point. That was when I knew he wasn't just eccentric. This was serious.

I asked him to see a psychiatrist. He agreed because he'd been having trouble sleeping. He told the doctor about the invention and how he was the most important person since Jesus Christ because of it. The doctor didn't say much. A week later a billing statement arrived. It had a DSM code on it. This was pre-Google, and since I knew what the DSM was, we went to the library to look it up. The DSM is the manual in which psychiatric diagnoses all have a code number for medical records.

The code was for paranoid schizophrenia. The question of this mysterious something that was wrong with him, that had fueled my delusions that terrible August night in 1993, was finally answered.

We stopped by his father's house after the library. The entrance to the house from the garage went into the kitchen. His father was there, drinking a cup of coffee. My husband said jovially, "I've just been diagnosed with paranoid schizophrenia." His father pointedly looked at me, then back at him. "*You're* schizophrenic?" he asked, baffled.

I don't remember who was in the house. By then he had a new stepmother. I think more than one person was in the adjoining living room, and he went in to tell them. I remained in the kitchen. I vaguely heard his voice telling them, and laughter in response.

Recently I discussed this with a therapist in the context of my family's response to my own diagnosis. I told my mother about it a year after I was diagnosed. She seemed dismissive about it, shrugging while she said, "If you were diabetic, you'd need insulin." I've seen that comparison made elsewhere, and while it isn't wrong, I was hurt by the sense that it simply wasn't important to her. In this way, our families paralleled each other. But in my case, I wanted it to be important. It took me a long while to understand that it was something of a joke to my husband. Perhaps to some degree his family's dismissal of it was in response to his own framing of it.

Years later, my mother saw me being symptomatic for the first and only time, and she did take it seriously then. I was glad she saw it wasn't something to shrug off.

Because of this diagnosis, I felt motivated to stay

and support him, to help him recover, or cope. Yet, like his family, I was in denial about him, too. Yes, he was mentally ill, but I wasn't convinced paranoid schizophrenia was an appropriate diagnosis. It seemed so extreme. But now that he was seeing a psychiatrist he could start to get better, and maybe we'd find a way to have a more normal life. He was thirty-nine years old when diagnosed.

He started seeing a therapist recommended by his father, who'd seen her when he was grieving the death of my mother-in-law. The therapist was a nurse practitioner, and at one point, I was seeing her too, separately. Her seeing both of us this way was probably extremely unethical, and kind of weird. It would have made more sense for us to see her together. If we had, I might have gotten a better sense of how ill my husband really was.

One week, I was crouched in front of the refrigerator, reaching for something on the bottom shelf, and I fell backwards a little bit in the awkward position. This happened twice in one week, just a normal awkward moment. The next week, she said, "You've been falling down? Something is wrong with your balance?" That was how my husband described it to her, that I had just started falling down for no reason. That was the only inkling I got from how grossly he might have been exaggerating my condition behind my back.

I was still very depressed, having a hard time being alone when my husband was at work at his delivery job for Airborne Express. My COBRA insurance had run out, and the only health insurance his job offered would cost fifty percent of his pay. Since he had this schizophrenia diagnosis, the therapist encouraged him to quit his job and accept disability. I wondered later if he could have just gotten a better job, for example, with UPS, since he had this delivery experience. But he also wanted to quit to be with me twenty-four hours a day because he felt he had to take care of me and keep me from committing suicide. His goal was to take care of me. His plan was that by decreasing our income, I'd qualify for Medicaid.

The disability checks for each of us were four hundred dollars a month. My memory is a little fuzzy, because at some point we delivered Pennysavers on the weekends for another four hundred. But once we got that Pennysaver job, our income was too high for Medicaid after all. Janssen Pharmaceuticals put me on a program to get their Risperdal for free at that point, in a program called Janssen Cares. It's easy to condemn Big Pharma, but I'm grateful they did that.

After a few months of this, I'd been on disability long enough to be put on Medicare.

I didn't know that I'd be eligible for Medicare after two years on disability. When I was about to lose my Medicaid, I had a decision to make. Though I was on risperidone by then, I was still taking lithium carbonate. Lithium causes a hole in the heart of the developing fetus. The question was whether I should go ahead and have a tubal ligation while I still had insurance to cover it. I was 35 years old. I was still thinking, though, that I might be schizophrenic. If I was, maybe there was no reason to take the lithium. I decided to have a psychiatric evaluation. It was a strange and useless experience.

I went back to the county clinic and met with a friendly male psychiatrist. He had an English accent and a pleasant demeanor. When I told him of my dilemma he said, "Ah, but pregnancy protects you." He seemed to think you don't become manic while pregnant, which I'm pretty sure isn't true. In terms of whether risperidone causes birth defects, they didn't know. He then asked me if my mom had any illness or health issues while she was pregnant with me. I replied, "I have a twin brother who isn't mentally ill."

"Ah, you're a thinker," he said.

From there a young woman—I'm not sure her professional capacity—gave me two psychiatric tests. One was a yes or no questionnaire that contained at least one very difficult question:

"Sometimes I like to just sit and stare into space."

This was impossible to answer yes or no to. I did often just sit and stare. But I didn't *like* to, not at all. I knew I was wasting time doing it. So how should I answer? Yes, because I did do this, or no, because I didn't *like* it? I don't remember how I answered.

The other was a Rorschach test. Immediately I noted the colors. The images are not black and white. I complimented the prettiness of the colors as I talked about what the shapes looked like.

A week later, I met with the young woman to discuss the results. She said, "We did see some psychotic elements in the tests." What? What was she talking about? There were obvious questions about paranoia I knew I got right, that I said no to. I didn't ask her to explain. When it came to the Rorschach test she said, "You only used the shape to determine the image, not the colors. This means you have difficulty getting along with people," or words to that effect. I protested that I did compliment the colors. She said yes, but I didn't use them.

That's all it led to. Whether I was schizophrenic still wasn't answered. The Rorschach test in particular seemed to me to be no better than astrology. I had the tubal ligation. On the operating table, before I was put under, I shed a few tears. The surgeon squeezed my arm to comfort me.

I didn't have a strong desire to be a mother. Of course having children with my first husband would have been a disaster. I was finally taken off lithium in 2000, since it never had much effect on me. At one point, a bit later, after my life changed dramatically for the better, I felt it might be nice to have a child, but that ship had sailed. It's not a tragedy.

I recently saw a play about a bipolar teenager, whose aunt has also been bipolar since adolescence as well. The fact that if you're diagnosed young, you're immediately told: you can't have children, was not mentioned in the play.

With the two disability checks, Medicare, and the Pennysaver job, we were getting by okay financially. Most years when the property tax was due, we happened to come into some money, such as the time the farmer down the hill logged some ash trees in our woods and shared the money with us. The main difficulty was keeping a car on the road, especially as the many miles over the hills every weekend took its toll.

We drove all afternoon and evening on Saturdays and Sundays with the Pennysavers, the landscape rolling by. The car radio barely got reception through the hills, and we'd struggle to listen to A Prairie Home Companion at six o'clock; sometimes all we could make out was the audience laughing.

One day I told the nurse practitioner how difficult our lives were. It was true that our income wasn't too bad, but we were still living on the margins of society. She said to me, "He just isn't taking good care of you, is he?" Since she was the one who pushed him to quit his job and go on disability, I wanted to slap her.

My husband liked to characterize me as writing crazy letters because of a few I sent while manic, so I was surprised by something that came in the mail then. We had a mortgage on our little house, and my husband got mad at the bank about something, I don't know what. One day when he wasn't home, I took in the mail. There was a letter he'd sent to our bank, which had been returned because he hadn't put a complete address on the envelope. I opened it. At the end of his complaint, he wrote, "This is why people blow up banks." My heart pounding, I thanked God it wasn't delivered. Would we have gotten a visit from the FBI? I'll never know. I didn't tell him the letter was returned. I don't know if there were any others like this.

A year went by after his diagnosis. Things didn't seem to change. There weren't signs he was getting better. I was starting to get frustrated with his doctors, because I felt they had given up on him, just didn't have a goal for him to get better. I even wrote an editorial about it and submitted it to NPR, for one of those human interest commentaries they used to run. Someone wrote back a personal reply, offering sympathy. That meant a lot. I think it was the only bit of sympathy anyone ever expressed to me during this whole scenario.

It must have been about 1997, he decided property taxes mean you don't really own your own home. Despite the fact that the house was still unfinished, he decided to build a boat in our yard for us to live on in Florida. I was still weak and passive. Maybe I thought the change would be good. Next to the house, I had only one little garden spot on the property. With the soil being like concrete, I'd put in a raised bed for flowers. He tore it all out because he needed that spot to build the boat.

CHAPTER SIXTEEN

It would be a sixteen by thirty-two foot catamaran, the two hulls each big enough for a full-size mattress in the back, spanned by an enclosed deck to be the living room and kitchen. The middle of the hulls were storage, with our old plastic camper toilet in the front end of one. A couple of steps led down to the hulls at each end. Sixteen by thirty-two was actually the size of one floor of our house, so this really was a pretty big, livable size.

He built the two hulls, eventually towing them to a marina on Lake Oneonta, and at the marina connected the hulls with the living space. It was all built of plywood. He painted it with blue marine paint, and I named it The Blue Heron.

At one point after he started all this, I had misgivings. It seemed a bit mad for someone who knew nothing about boats to do this. We were in the car driving somewhere, and I suggested he start by building a model boat. Maybe he could even build and sell model boats to raise the money. Exploding with anger, he cried out, "Burn the boat! Just burn the boat!" He rated whether people believed in the boat the same way he rated whether they believed in his Invention.

At this time, my father, now widowed by his second wife, was being bugged by someone in her family about the inheritance. I think it was her daughter's husband. Dad had five kids, but his wife only had two, so the son-in-law felt when he died it would be divided unfairly. To placate everyone, my dad sent everyone in the family a gift of five thousand dollars.

My husband put it all into the boat. I think sometimes what else we could have done. Fix the oven. Fix the chimney and have the wood stove again. Buy a lawn mower. Build a much needed garage.

Somehow, though, I passively went along with everything. Other than this somewhat depressed passivity, I was well enough to work, and eager to teach at last. It had been eight years since I'd graduated with my master's in education and teaching certificate. My twin brother's wife had an old friend who taught at a school in Tampa. They had an opening, and because I had that connection, they gave me the job. I was overjoyed. Tampa was the boating capital of the country. It seemed this was actually going to work out.

I moved there ahead of him. He took the boat to the Gulf through the Intracoastal Waterway, from Oneonta, New York, to Oldsmar, Florida. He wasn't alone at first. A friend of ours was with him for a while. I'm not sure at what point our friend left him to continue on his own.

He really did this. A big challenge was that he was mistaken about how big the engine needed to be, and the 9-horsepower motor barely got him through the tide under the Verrazano Bridge in New York City.

CHAPTER SEVENTEEN

I didn't teach long. I wasn't confident enough to discipline the kids, who were far younger than the ones I'd student taught. I taught sixth grade English, and seventh grade English and Geography. I was not qualified for this at all. Sixth grade was especially horrible, because the class is a mixture of children—really childish children—and hormonal adolescents. My training was for high school kids. It takes a very special personality to teach this age group, a personality that is not mine. I am cerebral. I want to do intellectual work with students. I'm not good at thinking up games and puzzles. I was also shocked to find that my seventh grade students, though this was a private school that gave the impression of academic rigor, were not at a high enough reading level to handle an article from *USA Today*.

I had an especially bad time with the principal. He was a disciplinarian, and it was his first year of being a principal, while he also taught math. Over time, I realized he was personally offended by my difficulties. I think he believed my inability to discipline was an act of willful disrespect on my part. One day, after I sent a particularly troublesome boy to the office (a boy who belonged in special ed), the principal stormed into my classroom. Red-faced and screaming, he shouted, "The next boy who is sent to my office will be expelled! EXPELLED!"

The boy in question was a difficult case. At the beginning of the year, we had a meeting with his grandmother and father who were raising him, the principal, and I forget which other teachers. The grandmother launched into a story of how in first grade he was exceptional, an A student, and they don't know what happened, but they were determined to keep him in regular school. I wanted to say, "I think he really needs special ed, and I do not feel qualified to teach him." But I didn't. Afterward, the principal said to me earnestly, "We have to help this kid."

By Thanksgiving, the dean of the school, a kindly priest, let me know the principal was asking people behind my back how he could break my contract and fire me. I quit and didn't come back after Christmas.

On my last day, I found out the principal had singled out that one boy who needed special ed, and told him he was to blame for my quitting. I remember the boy's sad, guilty face as he looked up at me apologetically, almost tearful. So much for, "We have to help this kid."

For many years afterward, I dreamt at night about wanting another chance, begging to be allowed to try to teach again. Sometimes I dreamt of chaotic classrooms running amok. Later I would dream I finally had a handle on it and did a good job. But I never taught again. The dreams have stopped coming now, but it took years.

There was one good moment in those awful months. A bee had gotten into the room. I handled it as my grandmother had taught me, by trapping it under a cup, sliding a stiff piece of paper under it, and letting it go out the window. A particularly sensitive, nature-loving boy was awestruck. He'd never seen anyone do this before. This was one special moment, and I do treasure that memory.

Around the time that I quit, my husband arrived with the boat (after a repair to the keel) in Oldsmar and I moved onto it. There was still only the porta-potty on the boat, and we used the dingy marina bathroom.

I was quite worried about what job I could be

qualified for, after failing as a teacher. I went to an employment office and they gave some weird, random test that led to nothing. They viewed me as having a master's degree and not someone who needed their help. In January, after looking for about three weeks, I got a job at a 24-hour copy shop. One night, one of my former students came in. Surprised to see me there, he asked if I was the manager. A little ashamed, I said no. But I didn't know I was hired because they were looking for an evening manager. The owner wanted to see how I worked out before offering it to me. So I became evening manager, after all. The man I replaced said they were impressed by something I'd written on my application form. The question was, "What do you like about working?" I had said, "Helping people." When I asked him what people usually wrote, he said, "Making money."

I was on my feet all day. We didn't have friends, the commute from the marina was long, and life was empty. To make a little extra money, my husband sold plasma once a week and enjoyed chatting with the other donors.

We both regularly saw a psychiatrist. Mine was for prescribing the risperidone that had worked so well in controlling my symptoms. I've never known what my husband's treatment consisted of then. Like me, he would just have a 15-minute appointment as if it were a medication check, but he wasn't prescribed medication, as far as I recall. I don't know what his psychiatrist's goal was in treating him. Nothing about him changed or got better. I wonder if I should have intervened, maybe attended his appointments with him, encouraged some kind of treatment. I continued to feel frustrated by what I thought was abandonment by his doctors, that they simply had no goal for him to get better.

It is only now, all these years later, that I understand. We were in touch last year, and at the time he was convinced he had a rare endocrine cancer. He shopped around for a doctor that would confirm his delusion, stubbornly insisting it was a "one in two hundred million case," and joking, "Paging Dr. House! LOL."

And I finally got it. This really is paranoid schizophrenia. And he never got better, not because it wasn't his doctor's goal, but because it wasn't *his* goal. He never intended to get better. He never intended to give up any of his delusions. His doctors probably did try to treat him, but he stubbornly refused to accept help, to accept reality.

At one point when we were still in New York, my sister mentioned that she had heard schizophrenics can be happy that way. This angered me at the time. I wanted to ask, Do you think we're happy? With this impoverished life on the margins of society? But now I see, yes, my husband was happy with his dysfunctional life. The poverty, the Pennysavers, none of this was a problem, not something to be solved. I was blind to that at the time.

When we were first together, he had a glow, an aura. He was charismatic. He also cared about my happiness in tender and thoughtful ways. One day we went to a Renaissance Faire. At a booth of gemstones and fossils, I was captivated by a crystalline fossil seashell. I felt we couldn't afford it. We separated for a few minutes as we looked around, and the next thing I knew, he rushed up and presented me with the shell. It was so sweet. I actually still have it.

Over that year in Florida, gradually that glow was gone. It seemed like he was always complaining, and involving himself in the dysfunctional, depressing lives of other people at the marina. One thing I'd noticed about him over the years was his tendency to befriend dysfunctional people: addicts, alcoholics. In this way he was always the most functional person in the room. I began to crave to be surrounded by successful, competent people, even if I was the least functioning, least successful person in the room.

I finally understand now, after all these years, why he changed, why his charm was gone and he only complained, no fun anymore. It was because he couldn't stand that I wasn't disabled. In one of the last exchanges we've had, over Facebook, he criticized me for no longer accepting disability. I said that because of my medication, I was no longer disabled. He replied, "Being dependent on medication is the very definition of disability." Of course, that's nonsense. But he couldn't bear the thought I wasn't disabled, and his grumpiness in Florida was because of that.

The 24-hour copy place where I worked was so dry, the cold air conditioning chapped my lips and I started sucking in my lips a lot, and licking them. I started to fear I was developing tardive dyskinesia, that side effect of antipsychotics. After being on them for six years, I started cutting my three milligram pills in half. I started to become mildly manic.

Working forty hours a week for a year with no

break for the first time was exhausting. I know other people do this, and I admire their stamina greatly. My husband and I talked about having me go back on disability, which I'd given up two years earlier. We'd declare bankruptcy on our credit card debt, even though we weren't in much debt at all, and take the boat back up North. That slightly manic week, I knew I had to leave. I had to find a normal life. I loaded up my little Neon, left a note, and drove to my mother's place in Ohio, a two-day trip. It was over.

When we were first engaged and I was in graduate school, I had said I was marrying him because "he makes my life easier." If I had to say in one sentence why I left, it would be, simply: he stopped making my life easier.

I got a dissolution rather than a divorce, because that meant he wouldn't have to appear in court. The hearing only took five minutes. I called him that night to tell him, and he said, "We'll exchange Christmas cards." For the next few years, we exchanged one or two letters a year.

I asked him once a few years after I left whether his family ever accepted his diagnosis.

He replied, "No. They blame you."

I'd really like to know if his family ever accepted it. At first, I didn't fully accept it either. After all, he didn't have hallucinations. People think with schizophrenia, that the person doesn't know what's real, is in a constant state of psychosis. No one imagines a schizophrenic can be charismatic and articulate.

He doesn't accept his diagnosis anymore either. Now his self-diagnosis is PTSD, believing his mother beat him when he was a child, and that the memory was repressed.

He's been fixing up another boat, mostly homeless, and posted on Facebook he was helping to hide a friend from the law. In December someone posted on his Facebook page that he had died. I thought, I guess it was cancer after all. I sent a note of condolence to his sister. A few weeks later he emailed me: "Not dead, not yet, unless someone forgot to tell me."

We exchanged a couple of emails. His test result that had inspired his cancer delusion was due to two harmless, small tumors in his liver. He was suffering from a low pulse rate called bradycardia which he believed could be fatal at any time. At fifty beats per minute, it was not actually dangerously low.

This story is a tragedy. He never got better. I've

almost never told anyone the rest of his story, about the boat, because I found it too depressing to talk about. After I left, he took his boat back up North. That was where I last saw him, when I returned to pick up some things I'd left. Later he tried returning South again. Around South Carolina, his engine died. Stranded, he had to tie the boat to a tree behind someone's house.

One day when he was off the boat, the owners of the house cut his line and let the boat drift away. It was eventually found by the Coast Guard being pushed by ice, and he surrendered it to them.

After living with his grandmother to take care of her, then his father to take care of him (until he died), he used a small inheritance to build another boat of the same design. It really looked impressive. He brought it down the Hudson to New York City and tied it to some kind of buoy at a marina. This was in the month of December. He had a girlfriend with him and they spent the night at her mother's apartment in Manhattan.

The next day when they returned to the marina, the boat had been swamped and sunk by ice. He had insurance, which covered the cost of hauling it out of the water and junking it. The girlfriend didn't stay with him much longer.

Now he's acquired another, smaller boat he's working to fix up in Maryland. His goal is to take it to the Virgin Islands. I worry he'll never survive the ocean voyage and hope he never attempts to make this fantasy come true.

He did see psychiatrists sporadically after I left, and tried medication. When he didn't like how he felt and stopped taking it, he ended up being briefly committed to a psych ward. It's been a while since then.

I wonder what his family thinks, if they think I drove him crazy. I caused so much stress and anger. It's behind me now, but when I see an angry, crazy, shouting person in the street, I can only think, *there but for the grace of God go I.*

And I can't help thinking now, over and over, what if I had stayed in the ward in Concord that day instead of leaving? And what if, when my husband said, "I *like* your tie," I had turned and said, "Tell the doctor about the Invention. Tell him all about it." Would his illness have come out three years earlier? Would that have made any difference? I keep daydreaming of that conversation.

I'd promised while in the ward I'd stay seven

more years, and coincidentally, I did. I said it's possible a small amount of good came out of staying those extra years. This is what I meant: Over time, I noticed his sister treating her young son with the kind of cold, critical manner that my husband had experienced with his mother. And her son started to develop an interest in discovering how to invent a free energy generator.

Soon after I left, I wrote to his sister with my concerns. I was honest about how I felt my husband had been treated, and that this might be a pattern. The very last time I saw her, when I returned to pick up some boxes I'd left behind in the boat, she was there. She gave me a big, surprising hug. Did I do some good? If so, I can forgive myself for staying. Maybe that was the fulfillment of the promise I'd made to his mother, when I sat with her body that day in 1992.

CHAPTER EIGHTEEN

In the early years, I needed to write to you. I was isolated, with no one to talk to about the stress and mystery of what was going on. After I remarried and my life improved, the habit to write to you was ingrained. And I loved you, terribly.

The obituary says you died "after a brief illness." I'll never know more. Are my letters in a big box somewhere? In perhaps the last letter you read from me, I suggested you donate them to an archive, as if I knew you were dying.

It seemed like we had a psychic connection. I once wrote you a description of what I thought your wife was like. That she had long brown hair down her back like the young Joan Baez. I felt you were urban in your roots, and she was a countrywoman in contrast. Later I learned you were from Baltimore, and I came across a photo of your wife on the Internet. She had long brown hair exactly as I'd described, and she was on a horse, a countrywoman. After three days, I knew you "that well."

In the beginning of this, there was no Google. I looked up your name in a surname dictionary at the library, and it was the Hebrew word for "contented," so I thought you were Jewish. Only long later, thanks to Google, did I learn it was a Polish name, and found you listed among alumni of a private Catholic school. I didn't intend to find out about your family, but your name is unusual, and I ended up seeing your kids in the local news, competing in high school sports. That's how I learned that when we met you probably had a toddler and a baby at home.

"A brief illness." I always thought that if you knew you were dying, maybe you'd write, just the one time, a letter to be delivered posthumously. A letter saying you were glad to hear from me, that you were proud of me.

Of course, you could never write back. How did you feel about my letters? Did they ever entertain you? Did I hound you? Were my letters like a cloud of Oresteia Furies?

I wrote to you about the happy turns in my life, about being reunited with my best friend from college and marrying him. The one we'd visited in Chicago, who disagreed with the physics of the lift disk idea, the one I'd enraged through our letter exchange, the man who I wrote to from Columbus after I left Florida to try to make up, who said come to Chicago for Thanksgiving when I wrote, who still lived with almost no furniture, into whose life I've now brought much furniture, who had been in love with me for twenty years, who had never dated, who said when I asked to kiss him that Thanksgiving that he didn't know how—and in the words of Charlotte Brontë: Reader, I married him. He brought me to live in a city for the first time in my life, where I thought I could never be happy, but now love so much I would never live anywhere else.

It's his family in Indianapolis who keeps asking, "Do you feel safe? Do you feel *safe* in Chicago?" Despite fantasizing all those years that you and I might end up together, I didn't hesitate. He is the only man on earth I wouldn't leave to be with you. That's saying a lot.

Once when I was eleven years old, my twin brother and I were walking with my aunt down a street in Cincinnati. My aunt was only twenty-four, and suddenly she took off and ran ahead of us to the corner. When we caught up, she said, "I had a sudden burst of energy."

I was amazed. I was in the middle of years of terrible insomnia, in a constant state of exhaustion. In candid photos of me as a teenager I look like a drug addict with such dark circles around my eyes. I couldn't imagine ever having a burst of energy. Now as I walk the sidewalks of Chicago, my pace is rapid, exactly three miles per hour, and I often take off running for no reason, in a burst of energy. I never thought I would feel so alive.

There was still some melancholy, because I longed for a professional identity, which eluded me for years. When I finally got a novel published after seventeen years of rejection, were you proud of me? I pictured you opening a bottle of champagne with your wife to celebrate, a toast I would never hear. All these years I felt your long-distance support.

I followed your career as you left the ward to go into providing TMS treatments for depression. Then one day, you weren't on your company website. Strange. I thought if you ever died, they would put a memoriam on the website, so I wasn't worried. I sent them an email to ask if you'd retired, and I thought, *yes, I can let go now, this is the end of the letters.*

After I sent the email, I went for a walk, headed to Buffalo Exchange to sell a skirt. Waiting my turn, I took out my phone. I'd missed a call, and listened to the voice mail. A woman said you'd recently passed away. I sat there, the store a dark buzz fading into the distance.

How can you be ashes now? I thought I'd see you once more, shake your hand goodbye, maybe give you a hug and feel the smooth fabric of your suit against my cheek. Your strong arms holding me, as they've been holding me for thirty years. How can your arms be ashes?

Writing to you made my life more real, a little bit bigger, a little more important. Now you are ashes, and I am anonymous.

In the last letter I mailed, I waxed philosophical. I had wondered for years whether to believe in God. It seemed ungrateful not to, and the universe fills me with such awe. I concluded: "It's enough to believe in Wonder. I believe in the wonder of the universe. The wonder is enough." That was the letter that probably arrived the day you died.

CHAPTER NINETEEN

Two nights after I first saw your obituary, I awoke from a nightmare that a dead body was in the room. My bed was in the kitchen, and a trash bag next to me held a body covered in coffee grounds. I remembered the tour of your ward the first day, how I pointed out to the nurse someone had dumped coffee grounds into the recycling bin. The body covered in coffee grounds in my dream echoed that image. As I lay awake, my heart pounding, it came to me, the understanding of why I couldn't stop writing to you for thirty years.

The truth was hidden from me all these years, and now it's obvious. I had come back to your ward that day, but was turned away because of the policy that I couldn't be re-admitted. I don't like using the word trauma, which I think gets overused, but being turned away was a kind of trauma.

I never got over the trauma of wanting to change

my mind and come back. All these years, I've wanted a second chance, a do-over. Every letter to you has been an attempt to have that conversation we never had. Every letter was that return.

Did you know this? Maybe you did. For thirty years I've wanted that do-over, that chance to talk it all over, to recover with you and show you my sane side. Today I know that I never got over this keen desire for a do-over, the chance to come back. And now I can't tell you this. I have to face the regret with a fresh ache in my chest.

As in New York, I go for long walks. Chicago has an astounding amount of nature along the river and in pockets of forest preserve. When I see woodpeckers in their bouncy flight, I show you. In spring when the melody of a white-throated sparrow calls with its eerie, human-like voice, we listen together. Herons glide before us in Gompers Park. Silent, a mystery, you are in my eyes, admiring all the birds.

I had another dream last night, about something I'd forgotten, even though it was the most important reason I was in love with you.

All those years ago, when we lived surrounded by alcoholics and drug addicts, I craved being among successful people, even if I were the least successful, least competent person in the room.

After moving to Chicago to marry my dear old friend, I gradually got involved in theater and creative projects. Bit by bit, I learned how to be a leader. I'm still learning, of course. Each project has been a little more ambitious.

On one project in particular, I had a very stressful time. Part of that stress revolved around being afraid to assert myself. I felt intimidated, and couldn't put myself forward to tell someone what I needed from them. I was losing sleep, getting emotional, almost delusional with stress.

But one day I knew this couldn't go on. Trembling with anxiety, I made a phone call I had to make, and expressed the direction I felt the project needed. And to my surprise, relief, even joy, it was not a problem. It was perfectly okay. There was no reason for this anxiety at all. I had made it all stressful because of my own lack of confidence and feeling of intimidation.

And in that moment, a lifetime of anxiety lifted from my shoulders. I realized that there was never any reason to feel this fear, this dread of asserting myself. That it's okay just to tell someone, this is what is needed, this is what we need to do.

Over the years, I've spent many hours discussing in therapy my wish to feel like an adult. I always felt small, less than. Sometimes when I needed to assert myself, I felt as if I were submerged under water, so that I couldn't open my mouth to speak. Part of the reason I didn't feel like an adult was simply a lack of life experience. I hadn't been employed much, or socialized much. I didn't have opportunities for the kind of growth most people get in young adulthood. This stressful project became an abrupt and urgent need to grow up and solve problems, because if I didn't get a handle on it, it would be a disaster for me and everyone on the team.

The stress continued, even escalated, because a lot was going wrong. I was putting out fires right and left. With the dread and anxiety of facing problems now over, my new strength and confidence had come just in time to keep me going and solve the problems that arose. In the end, the project was a big success, and no one on the team even knew all the stress it was for me.

Then I had a dream last night, and it triggered a memory of why you meant so very much to me. It was because when I was with you, in that short time of only three days, I felt an enormous sense of equality with you. So often in my life I've felt inferior, at other times superior, too, because I put everyone on a scale, measuring myself against everyone I met. But with this challenging project completed, I feel very differently. For the first time, I don't have to feel intimidated by anyone ever again. I can face challenges that would have scared me before, and can assert myself because the fear all along was only a bogey man, a trick I'd played on myself. Now it's hitting me, it's because inferior and superior are delusions. If someone knows more than me or has more experience, I can learn from them. And if I happen to know a little more than someone else, I can help them. Inferior and superior are delusions, ideas we make up to feel bad about ourselves, judgments that must be shed like a false skin.

I can go through the world feeling equal, the way you made me feel. That was the gift I needed from you, that you gave me, such as the moment when you said, "You're reading too much into things," like a fellow adult, and maybe some other moments I no longer remember. I only had an inkling of this, until my dream last night. When I awoke, all this became clear.

The dream: I was in a gym with a group of women who were exercising in red uniforms, widely spread over a vast space, the air dimly glowing with a foggy light. They were tossing an orange back and forth to each other over a great distance. I have never caught a ball in my life, and I wanted very much to catch one. From far away, beyond where I could see, an orange came toward me. I caught it perfectly. I knew you were in charge of this gym, and I was eager to tell you. You had to be there somewhere, and I found you, looking as you had that night thirty years ago, with your big brown eyes behind glasses, dark blond hair, a face that was soft with sympathy, so tall, and though I never hugged you, your broad-shouldered presence was like a comforting hug.

Thrilled at my success, I excitedly told you I caught the orange.

In a soft, kindly voice, you replied, "Who do you think threw it to you?"

Thank you.

Love,

A

ABOUT THE AUTHOR

Amy Crider is an award-winning novelist and playwright who has won honors for both fiction and drama. Born in Ohio and raised in rural upstate New York, she studied theater at Goddard College and later trained at Second City and Chicago Dramatists. Her work explores themes of redemption, courage, and compassion. She lives in Chicago.